THE GOSPEL UNADORNED

Deconstructing the Religious Church

ISBN (978-0-646-86260-6)

Published by The Core Media Group, Inc., www.thecoremediagroup.com

Cover & interior layout designed by Emily Morelli, www.bluemusestudo.com

Edited by Chuck Johnson

Printed in the United States of America.

THE GOSPEL UNADORNED

Deconstructing the Religious Church

JOHN CLEMENTS

DEDICATION

To my beloved, my one and only love, my wife Vivien who passed away to be with the Lord just before I began writing this book. Isaiah 57:1-2.

*I have quoted wording from the New International Version of the Bible (NIV) where possible. Where I have considered it essential to understanding, I have also quoted Greek text. Where it occurs in the Old Testament, I have quoted from the Septuagint, a translation into Greek from the original Hebrew dated around 400BC. I consider this a very reliable rendering of the Hebrew as it reflects the understanding of Jewish scholars of the time. Where I have quoted Greek in the New Testament, I have used the words as they appear in the original New Testament manuscripts. Wherever I have used Greek letters for a word, I have also provided a transliteration into English.

CONTENTS

INTRODUCTION

The Gospel Unadorned is offered primarily to mature Christians for stimulation of discussion and for challenging long-held assumptions about how to "do church." But I rather hope that those who have been put off Christianity by what they have perceived as the church may also read it and will delight in my offering. Perhaps they may even embrace the Christian faith at last. I offer this book in all humility as a work I have been convicted to write. I am more than willing to hear refutations of any or all the points I make. But if I am right about any part of this book, it means that God is waiting to undertake a seismic shift in the way we Christians do things.

I was brought up in a "blended" family—my father was a Methodist and my mother an Anglican! As a child I attended both churches, but that hardly gives me the basis for writing this book. In my adult life I worshiped at an Evangelical church where I became an elder for many years. But the nearest I have come to documented theological qualification is a certificate of clinical pastoral education (CPE), allowing me to function as a chaplain and to express my principal gifting in pastoral ministry. I have a heart for the lost sheep. I am not a theologian and am not an ordained minister. I am, however, a Royal Priest[1], and proudly proclaim such. I am also an academic and physician and have relied on that training to shape my writings in this book.

Not all Christians have got everything wrong. To suggest that would be shameful and incorrect. There have been martyrs and amazing church leaders over the centuries who have forged a way toward God and his redemption. But I do want to consider that we, the body

---

[1] For a discussion on the Royal Priesthood of all believers, see Chapter 6.

of Christ, have often unwittingly been blown off course and are in danger of drifting even further off course with time. While I have tried to identify elements of church life that I consider inappropriate, I have also included elements that should be kept at all costs, such as the appointment of elders and Holy Communion.

If you don't like the way this is going, if you don't want to be challenged in your practice of your Christian faith, if you are completely content with your status, stop reading now, because this book is not for you!

To justify my stance on a given point, I have quoted scripture wherever possible, and some may claim I have misused or misinterpreted quotes. But where I have expressed my personal opinion, I have prefaced the comments with "I believe" or "I think." These are the points at which you can shout at me if you disagree!

The very last thing I want to do is to make Christians reading this short book feel that I am condemning them.

> *"Therefore, there is now no condemnation for those who are in Christ Jesus." (Romans 8:1).*

If God has placed you in a position, even as a leader in a conventional church, you are where He wants you to be. It is not for me to condemn anyone, especially those responding to God's plan.

The situation for the Israelites was very different. From the moment they were given the Law (Exodus 20), they were under condemnation. They were unable to keep every letter of the Law. Instead of their just punishment for sin—death—they were told about substitutionary sacrifice whereby an animal's blood was spilt at the altar in their place. There was no forgiveness without the spilling of blood. The Cross changed everything. The system of temple sacrifice was abolished, and Jesus became the substitutionary sacrifice, once and for all, not dying again and again for each of our sins. We are no longer under condemnation, but by faith alone in Jesus alone, we receive forgiveness and redemption.

If you accept Jesus as your Saviour, you have redemption. You were justified at the point of conversion, and you have been undergoing sanctification ever since then. Our process of sanctification will continue until our death when we will be resurrected with Christ in a new, glorified body. And I am at the front of the queue needing forgiveness through undeserved grace. When we come before the great white throne of judgment as glorified individuals, justified by our faith in Jesus, we will be judged as *individuals,* not in groups nor by denomination! We are each responsible for ourselves and for no one else. Scripture tells that every one of us is a sinner and in need of God's forgiveness. We as *individuals* must repent and seek God's forgiveness, relying on His grace.

The target of this book is not about *individual* condemnation or *individual* salvation. There are much more learned books than this one on such matters. Instead, I have felt the need to focus on the *corporate* manifestation of the body of Christ, the *ekklesia*[2]. It is this corporate expression that I am interested in. Old Testament prophets continually called for *corporate repentance* by the entire nation of Israel. Ezekiel pointed to the leaders (he called them the shepherds) of Israel, calling them to *corporate* repentance because they were not protecting the sheep from the wolves (Ezekiel 34).

If we are responsible before God for our own personal behaviour and faith in Jesus, do we also have any responsibility for how the *ekklesia* behaves? I propose the answer to be yes. What happens in the *ekklesia* does not happen in isolation from the individual; indeed, the *ekklesia* is made up of individuals. If every individual believed in the reality of the priesthood of all believers, for instance, then the *ekklesia* would be transformed into a no-clergy-no-ordained-priest expression. Can we make such radical changes that would cause that to happen?

Is God indifferent to the state of the *ekklesia*? By no means. God is shaking Christianity's religious foundations and will continue to

[2] For an explanation of *ekklesia*, see Chapter 4.

do so until the *ekklesia* reverts to what God desires, either gradually or suddenly.

My intention is to challenge long-held beliefs and to encourage us all to rethink elements of Christian practice that may not properly honour our Maker. I discuss "deconstructing" or "dismantling" the church, words that will annoy, distress, and confuse many.

I have taken the image of deconstruction from Zechariah 3:3: "Now Joshua (the high priest) was dressed in filthy clothes as he stood before the angel. The angel said to those who were standing before him. 'Take off his filthy clothes.' Then he said to Joshua, 'See, I have taken away your sin and I will put rich garments on you.'" I believe God wants the filthy clothes of sin stripped off the religious church. And afterwards the body of Christ, the *ekklesia*, will be seen in all its glory and simplicity. I offer the suggestion that God may be wanting a complete, radical rethink about how we do church, starting again from the gospel unadorned—faith alone in Jesus alone.

Tell me I'm wrong. Tell me where I'm wrong.

John Clements
Australia

1

IS THERE A DOCTOR IN THE HOUSE?

The religious church system is sick.

I have already stated that I am no theologian. But I do have a medical background. I was a clinical paediatrician for a number of years before moving into Public Health where I spent the rest of my career. In both my clinical and public health work in developing countries, I employed a particular discipline that I consider is applicable to this book. I believe the religious church system is sick and applying a physician's approach might be insightful. We can take a good medical history, asking about symptoms, examine the facts and make a diagnosis before thinking about the treatment or remedy. Too often we jump from the initial symptoms to self-medicating the symptoms without addressing the underlying cause.

The symptoms of diarrhoea are some of the most common, often life-threatening problems in developing countries, especially among infants and children. Taking a history of the situation, we find that the problem starts with the parents—how they provide a sanitary environment for their infant, and how they find a source of clean water for domestic use. A sample of drinking water might be tested to find the likely organism contaminating the water and causing the diarrhoea. The diagnosis is easy—drinking water contaminated with *E. coli* bacterium. The solution is not so easy. The greatest impact is not from medicines that can provide only a temporary solution. No, the bulk of the solution lies in correcting human behaviour. For instance, avoiding shitting into the source of your drinking water. Pardon my directness. When a community has behaved in a particular way for generations, it is not easy to change their behaviour and "normalize" the new behaviour.

Another example might be lung cancer. We now know that smoking is the cause, but it took some clever studies to prove it. It is likely that individuals started smoking because they saw their parents smoking so the behaviour was "normal." Or they were influenced by peer pressure or the wider public behaviour that made it "normal" to smoke, even in the face of medical information that they chose to ignore or suppress. Again, the treatment was to change smoking behaviour across generations.

If you accept the possibility that this medical approach might reveal something insightful about the religious church, let us continue. What symptoms might be afflicting the church? Remember, the symptoms are only an indicator of the underlying cause of the illness. Can we get to the root causes, and can we devise solutions that may involve behaviour changes? Clearly not every church will be experiencing the same symptoms. But we can generalize to some extent.

SYMPTOM: ***Insufficient resources.***

EXAMINATION: Churches are always looking for resources to run the church and pay the pastor. If there is any left after that, maybe it can be given to missions.

ROOT CAUSE: A misunderstanding that Christians must always worship in a dedicated church building and must have paid staff to run it. Neither is correct. Giving in the New Testament was always about meeting other people's needs e.g., widows and orphans.

SYMPTOM: Perpetuating traditions.

EXAMINATION: Everyone knows what the Sunday church service is all about and willingly goes along with tradition.

ROOT CAUSE: So much of what we have assumed all our lives to be "normal church" is in fact tradition passed on to us from previous generations of churchgoers. And these traditions may or may not be scriptural. However, because we have grown up with them and have seen our parents do it, we assume it is the proper response to being a good Christian. This mindset is at the root of many elements of the religious church that I am now challenging. The origin of many of these traditions is examined in Chapter 7. *Pagan Traditions*.

Symptom: ***Burnt-out clergy.***

Examination: The clergy do practically everything and the congregation is passive.

Root cause: Incorrect understanding of clergy and laity, and linked to that, the belief that ordained priests are trained to run churches and *should* run churches. There is no understanding of the priesthood of all believers. I deal with this in Chapter 6. *The ordained priesthood dismantled.* I also discuss the shaking of the church in Chapter 15 when God will shake us all awake.

Symptom: Poor or incomplete understanding of the scriptures.

Examination: Many congregations are limited to Sunday sermons for scriptural teaching and understanding. People are rocked when difficulties come and are easily blown off course. They have not been taught properly that difficulties will arise, and they must be ready to stand firm. They are not willing to follow Christ whatever the cost.

Root cause: Clergy and laity are stuck on the idea that the sermon is the principal teaching tool and an essential part of Christianity. I deal with this in Chapter 7. *Pagan traditions*, where I discuss the pagan origins of the sermon and its use as a teaching method. In Chapter 19, I discuss alternative interactive teaching methods in, for example, house churches.

Symptom: Dependence on meeting in church buildings once a week.

Examination: Sunday services have been a tradition for centuries. Every Christian is expected to go to church on Sunday and dress in their Sunday best. We always have done it that way.

Root cause: An incorrect understanding of what the church is and what the *ekklesia* is.

I explain the true meaning of the *ekklesia* in Chapter 4. *The Ekklesia*, and the abolition of temple worship in Chapter 5. *The Temple*.

Symptom: Inappropriate leadership.

Examination: Those appointed to leadership within a church may promote themselves to a higher status than the laity.

Root cause: There is a misunderstanding of the principle of servant-leader. I deal with the appointment of leaders in Chapter 8. *Elders, Bishops and Deacons*, and Chapter 9. *The Fivefold Ministry*, explaining the importance of servant leadership and spiritual gifts.

Symptom: Minimal or no outreach or evangelism.

Examination: Congregations are passive.

Root cause: The wider Christian community often sees outreach or evangelism as the task of professional staff or those specially gifted. Or they may feel untrained or inadequate for the task. In Chapter 10. *The Great Commission*, I deal with how we can all evangelize in our daily lives.

Symptom: Lack of unity between churches/denominations.

Examination: As many as 45,000 denominations are thought to exist.

Root cause: Some denominations have been formed out of a genuine desire for presenting a better version of the gospel. Others have been formed out of pride and rebellion. Even sharing the basic tenets of Christianity does not seem to be enough to bring denominations together in unity. I deal with this in Chapters 12 and 13 on *Denominations* and *Ecumenism*, discussing how the church has split into so many fragments and why.

Symptom: Ordinary Christians follow unscriptural theologies.

Examination: People are misled into false teaching by false teachers, some forming sects.

Root cause: Because there is no opportunity for discussion during formal teaching, we are not encouraged to question what we are taught. But even those who should be able to discern the truth can be misled by clever teachers who lead people into wrong thinking. I deal with this in Chapter 14. *False Teachers*.

Symptom: Lonely people.

Examination: People arrive at Sunday church lonely and an hour later leave the church still lonely. This applies as much to mega-churches with congregations in thousands as it does to smaller churches of only fifty.

Root cause: The Sunday service rarely provides the appropriate context for intimate contact that is needed to overcome loneliness. I discuss some ways the *ekklesia* can meet the needs of lonely people in Chapter 19. *House Churches*.

Symptom: The congregation is composed mostly of women and the clergy composed mostly of men.

Examination: Women have been excluded from ministry in every denomination until very recently, and even now are unable to function on an equal footing to men in many church settings.

Root cause: Men have wanted to maintain dominance over women in all spheres of life including the church. In Chapter 20. *Women in ministry*, I look at the scriptural basis for women teaching and functioning equally with male believers.

Symptom: Praying to Mary and the saints.

Examination: More than half of all Christians pray to Mary and the saints.

Root cause: Catholic theology has developed over the centuries to espouse doctrines proposed by the Papacy. These may not be in accordance with scripture but are taught to be correct by the religious church. In Chapter 22. *Blown off course*, I discuss the issue of believing in Jesus alone as our Redeemer alongside adopting practices and theologies that are not scripturally based.

Symptom: Dwindling numbers in the congregation.

Examination: Mostly older generations coming to church on a Sunday.

Diagnosis: The younger generations are put off by what church offers. They seek alternative expressions of spirituality that they think are more attractive than the religious church.

Root cause: The religious church offers religious church, not the simple, unadorned gospel.

I deal with this issue in Chapter 23. *Why do people get put off by the Gospel??*

Symptom: The comfortable church.

Examination: Western culture has been allowed to infiltrate the church.

Root cause: We are constantly striving towards comfort in the church. This includes comfy seats, coffee shop, even squash courts and other sports facilities. We do not know what it is to suffer with Christ, because our comfort makes us immobile.

Each of these issues is dealt with in more detail in the remainder of the book.

2

WHO IS A CHRISTIAN?

If they were asked, a proportion of individuals in Western countries would say that they were Christian. But are they really? For many it just means that they live in a country that has traditionally considered itself to be Christian and that they live a "good life." They may even feed the poor on Friday night and go to church on Sunday.

I have bad news for them: those actions alone do not qualify them! Then what does?

I like to think of Christianity as both very easy and very difficult. The easy part is that God has given us a free gift of salvation simply by having faith alone in Jesus alone for the forgiveness of our sins. This is the good news or "gospel." It is that easy. It is described as *justification.*

The difficult part is how we express this faith in our daily lives. The Bible gives us clear guidance on this. We are not saved by works. No. But as a result, the genuine believer is beset by greater challenges than any other world religion, being encouraged to live by faith alone and, among other difficult commands, to love our enemies.

THE APOSTLES' CREED

Several assumptions underpin justification by faith alone. These are superbly summarised in the Apostles' Creed ("creed" simply meaning belief—Latin=credo). It is a masterpiece of prose that was written around the fourth century AD, not composed by the Apostles but representing their teachings.

I believe in God, the Father almighty, creator of heaven and earth.

I believe in Jesus Christ, his only Son, our Lord, who was conceived by the Holy Spirit and born of the virgin Mary. He suffered under Pontius Pilate, was crucified, died, and was buried; he descended to hell. The third day he rose again from the dead. He ascended to heaven and is seated at the right hand of God the Father almighty. From there he will come to judge the living and the dead.

I believe in the Holy Spirit, the holy catholic church, the communion of saints, the forgiveness of sins, the resurrection of the body, and the life everlasting. Amen.*

*i.e., the true world-wide Christian church.

Paul explains in Romans how we become righteous before God at the moment we accept faith in Jesus (in Christian jargon known as the moment of conversion), the faith that our sins were borne and wiped away by the sinless one when he was crucified on the cross. Paul calls this JUSTIFICATION. For anyone to even want to be righteous before God requires an understanding that there is only one God, and He created the universe. It also requires an understanding that the entire humankind has a propensity to sin.

> "All of us have become like one who is unclean, and all our righteous acts are like filthy rags." (Isaiah 64:6).

We also need to accept that some part of us will outlive, in some way or form, the death of our human body. If you believe that we die in a puff of cosmic smoke and that is the end of us, the obvious consequence of that belief is hedonism, the living of life without the need to consider consequences, living in the moment.

If we believe in an existence after death, whatever form that may take, our life on Earth must have consequences. The afterlife could, in simplistic terms, be either "nice" or "not nice." The Bible explains that the "nice" and the "not nice" both last for eternity, in other words, quite a long time! How do we ensure that we join the group that enjoys the "nice" outcome? Here, the concept of judgment is described in the Bible when we all must stand before God on Judgment Day. The sheep will pass into everlasting paradise (whatever that looks like), while the goats progress to everlasting suffering (whatever that looks like). But for both, it is everlasting.

The crucial question is what determines whether we are sheep or goats. In its simplest terms, if we are found to be sinners by God, we will be consigned to the goats. We have already established that *everyone* is a sinner, so what hope have we? The answer is that on conversion (*we were justified by faith alone in Jesus alone*), we appear before God as justified and sinless, and we are assigned as sheep to everlasting paradise.

If you are still determined to identify yourself as a Christian, a person who has faith in Jesus Christ, in subsequent chapters I shall challenge you about *how* you express that Christianity. This short book is not principally an attempt to convert the reader, rather to challenge those who already consider themselves to be Christians and to propose that we may have been *doing church* all wrong for around 1900 years. If you agree with my propositions, we all need to change from our practice of religion to a faith alone in Jesus Christ alone. To do this, we may have to dismantle many of the elements of church into their simplest components before we can begin to build it up again as God would have it.

REFLECTIONS

What do you think are the qualities of a real *Christian?*

What elements of your faith might be misplaced?

3

THE UNDERLYING PROBLEM—FAITH VERSUS RELIGION

In the previous chapter, I implied that Christianity is a religion. It is NOT! It is a FAITH. The Bible does not ask us to build a religion; rather, it invites us to have faith in Jesus. What this book attempts to do is to show how men and women over the centuries have modified this simple truth and forced the faith to become a religion. Consequently, terrible things have been done in the name of the church that have soured the perception of the world against the faith of Christianity. You may have thought that faith and religion were pretty much the same. Well, let me tell you—in my opinion, they are NOT! They are profoundly different. Let us look at each one.

RELIGION

Religion is a belief in a god or gods and the resulting activities that underpin this belief. These might include praying or worshiping in a building such as a church, temple or mosque as well as other rituals. It is a particular set of belief and activities within a system. The word *religion* is found in the New Testament in only three places: the Book of Acts, the letter of Paul to the Galatians, and the book of James. In all three places the word is referring to Judaism, not Christianity. None the less, most authorities would lump Christianity along with Judaism, Islam, Hinduism and Buddhism as the five great religions of the world. The Abrahamic religions (Judaism, Christianity and Islam) take steps to ensure that beliefs and activities are properly maintained through the oversight of the priest, making a clear distinction between the priestly class and the laity.

God does not inhabit religion.

FAITH

Christian faith is faith alone in Jesus alone. Above all else, it involves a relationship with Abba Father, our creator God who loves us so much that He sent His only son to redeem us. It is Jesus' sacrifice on the cross that takes away our sins. Without a faith in Jesus and what he did for us, we are lost sheep.

> Now faith is the assurance of things hoped for, the conviction of things not seen. (Hebrews 11:1).
>
> And without faith it is impossible to please God, because anyone who comes to God must believe that He exists and that He rewards those who earnestly seek Him. (Hebrews 11:6).
>
> For by grace you have been saved through faith. And this is not your own doing; it is the gift of God, not a result of works, so that no one may boast. (Ephesians 2:8).
>
> For in the gospel the righteousness of God is revealed—a righteousness that is by faith from first to last, just as it is written: The righteous will live by faith. (Romans 1:7).

Too many people believe that because they practice a form of religion, they also belong to the Christian faith. Sadly, this is not the case. Many individuals who go to church on Sunday, perhaps even more than once in the day, are confident this alone qualifies them to call themselves Christian, with all the accompanying blessings. Beware.

> On that day many will say to me, 'Lord, Lord, did we not prophesy in your name, and cast out demons in your name, and do many mighty works in your name?' And then will I declare to them, 'I never knew you; depart from me, you workers of lawlessness.' (Matthew 7:22-23).

It is only by faith in Jesus that we can enter the Kingdom of God. All the pomp and ceremony of the high church, all the rules invented by men, mean nothing to God.

> "You do not delight in sacrifice, or I would bring it; you do not take pleasure in burnt offerings. The sacrifices of God are a broken spirit; a broken and contrite heart, oh God you will not despise." (Psalm 51).

> Sacrifice and offering you did not desire, but my ears you have pierced; burnt offerings and sin offerings you did not require. (Psalm 40).

> I have no need of a bull from your stall or of goats from your pens, for every animal of the forest is mine, and the cattle on a thousand hills. (Psalm 50).

It is clear from these verses that God is not wanting religious practices. The system of temple sacrifice and worship was comprehensively abolished. Yet we have almost completely reinstated it with our own version. God is looking, instead, for a humble and contrite heart and a faith in His son Jesus.

In the Book of Romans, Paul explains at length about justification, sanctification and glorification through faith in Jesus. He is referring to the individual who is justified before God the moment he/she accepts Jesus as his/her saviour. There is then a period of progressive sanctification as we continue to sin but draw nearer to "sainthood," which we do not reach until we pass through death to the next life. At that point we assume our glorified bodies.

This analogy works for the church as well. I believe God created the church at Pentecost and He accepts that it will be imperfect until the Day of Judgment, but the reality is that there will be an ongoing process of course correction until then. Let us be humble and accept those course corrections as they happen. We are already justified. Let us revel in the knowledge that God is still working on His church to sanctify us.

In subsequent chapters, we will explore in detail how the Christian faith has been hijacked and has become a religion, no longer a faith. But God has plans for its redemption.

REFLECTIONS

Can you see the stark difference between religion and faith?

What would it take for you to make a course correction in the way you practice your faith?

4

THE EKKLESIA

In the previous chapter, I examined the difference between faith and religion. Now I want to look at the word "church" and the meaning we give it. It may sound boring and even irrelevant to some Christians to delve into the original meaning of words, but in this case, it is vital. We have been accustomed to using the word "church" as an integral part of Christian conversation (I go to church on Sundays; the Church of England; the Catholic Church etc.). But by misunderstanding the word's origin, an incorrect stream of thinking has emerged. Our entire concept of the Church of Christ has been distorted.

So, where did the word "church" come from? First, we must start with a Greek word *ekklesia*. *Ekklesia* is derived from klesis = a calling (in life) and ek = out. Thus, the nearest translation into English is *the called-out ones*.

In ancient Greece, a ruling assembly of citizens—an *ekklesia*—was appointed as part of a democratic (the rule of the people) process to govern its city states. As Rome came into ascendency, it copied Greece and created a Conventus Civium Romanorum. This occurred when a group of Roman citizens as few as two or three were gathered anywhere in the world, it constituted the conventus as a local expression of Rome, the Roman equivalent of *ekklesia*. The word and concept were well understood by 300BC when the Septuagint translation of the Hebrew Old Testament into Greek was created. Here is the earliest use of the word *ekklesia* in the Greek Scriptures. The word emerges in the

Septuagint as the translation into Greek of the Hebrew word "*qahal*." This word comes from "*qol*" which means "voice" and thus "call" or "summon". The Septuagint translates it as *ekklesia*.

In Deuteronomy 4:10, God spoke through Moses to the people, saying, "Remember the day of assembly *(ekklesia)* you stood before the Lord your God at Horeb, when He said to me, "Assemble (*ekklesia-sou)* the people before me to hear my words so that they may learn to revere me as long as they live in the land and may teach them to their children." This day of assembly was a specific day when God called the people together and gave them the law.

Moses again reminded the people of this special day later in Deuteronomy: "God will raise up for you a prophet like me from your own brothers. You must listen to him. For this is what you asked of the Lord your God at Horeb (Mount Sinai) on the day of assembly." (Deuteronomy 18:15). There is clearly something important for us to understand about both the idea of the *ekklesia* and its association with a special day.

Moses was meeting with the people of Israel who had been *called out* of Egypt and were in the wilderness for 40 years. In Biblical symbolism, Egypt, Babylon, and Sodom all represent the corrupt world. We know that there were no permanent buildings in the wilderness in which the Israelites were wandering. They lived in tents and even the tabernacle was partly made of tenting. When Moses met the *ekklesia*, he was meeting with the people. There was no reference to a building. Indeed, there was no building capable of holding all the twelve tribes!

In Acts 7:38, Stephen is being accused before the Sanhedrin. He refers back to Deuteronomy 18:15 and this passage becomes the bridge between the OT and the NT. He changes one word—no longer the *day* of assembly, now it is "the assembly *in the wilderness*, with the angel who spoke to him on Mount Sinai, and with our ancestors; and he received living words to pass on to us." That phrase "assembly in the wilderness/desert" was written as εκκλησια εν τη ερημο—*ekklesia en ter eremo* (literally the congregation/assembly in the wilderness). Stephen was referring to the *ekklesia* in Moses' day as the Israelites wandered in the desert for 40 years. But I think he was also being prophetic when he saw that the *ekklesia* would indeed be in the metaphorical desert in years to come.

There is another fascinating reference to the church in the wilderness, this time in Revelation 12. Here there is a vision of a woman clothed with the sun, with the moon under her feet; and a crown of twelve stars on her head. This is a reprise of Joseph's dream in Genesis 37 where the stars are the twelve tribes of Israel, and the woman is Israel. Revelation tells of the woman, Israel, who is escaping to the desert where she is kept safe from the attack of Satan. This is surely an account of God's safeguarding His *ekklesia* in the desert in times to come. I believe John's vision is about present and future times for the *ekklesia* that will be difficult, maybe even persecuted, but we can rely on God to provide a refuge in our wilderness, just as He brought Israel out of the wilderness into the Promised Land.

The words *synagogue* and *ekklesia* are very similar in meaning. A synagogue was and is a building where a Jewish congregation assembles for worship and other religious observances. The word is derived from two Greek words "sun" meaning together and "agein" to bring. It is essentially a meeting place. The oldest synagogue building yet uncovered by archaeologists is the Delos Synagogue, a possibly Samaritan synagogue that dates from 150 to 128 BC, or earlier, and is located on the island of Delos, Greece.

Some scholars think that the destruction of Solomon's Temple in Jerusalem in 586 BC gave rise to synagogues after private homes were temporarily used for public worship and religious instruction. Whatever their origin, synagogues flourished side by side with the ancient Jewish Temple practices and existed long before animal sacrifice and the priesthood were brought to an end by the destruction of the Second Temple in 70AD. Thereafter, synagogues took on an even greater importance as the unchallenged focal point of Jewish religious life. However, the first century Christians did not follow the Jewish model of building a sacred place, even though many would have been Jewish. They met as the *ekklesia* in homes.

Christians had been persecuted in the Roman Empire since Nero in 54AD. None the less, the faith flourished in the face of this persecution. When Emperor Constantine converted the Roman Empire to Christianity, he then controlled the secular and the religious sectors of the Empire. A hierarchical system soon followed, thereby consolidating the authoritarian rule by the clergy. In so doing, he perverted the faith into a religion based largely on Pagan practices. Services were to be held in specifically dedicated buildings under the authority of the clergy. Any idea that the people should be free to meet in private homes without supervision was gone. The *ekklesia* was now firmly established as the Roman Catholic Church, giving a new meaning to the word "*church.*".

When King James ordered an English translation of the Bible, he directed the translators on several issues. He wanted the translation to make clear that the Anglican Church was *the church*, and he was the boss of all the clergy and all the people (by God's appointment according to the understanding of the times). Thus "*ekklesia*" was translated as "church" with all the accompanying significance that word had then and now. Unexpectedly, the word for church in Spanish is *iglesia*, and in French *église*, both clearly derived from *ekklesia*. But these words have long since been inextricably linked to the building and the system, and they only apply to the Roman Church. A Protestant church in France is "un temple", denigrating it to the level of the pagan temple!

King David wrote about the great assembly in Psalm 40. He said: "I proclaim righteousness in the great assembly" (verse 9) and "I do not conceal your love and your truth from the great assembly" (verse 10). In both cases he uses *en ekklesia megaler* (εν εκκλησια μεγαλη). I think he was imagining how he would praise God in the assembly of Israelites when they came together, for example, during the great feasts in Jerusalem. But as so often with Psalms of David, he manages to move subtly into Messianic prophecy, guided by the Holy Spirit. In the case of the great assembly, I believe God was showing him, albeit darkly, an image of end times, of the great day of the last feast of Tabernacles. “During the Feast of Tabernacles when all Israel comes together (*ekklesiasas*) to appear before the Lord your God at the place He will choose, you shall read the law before them in their hearing.” (Deuteronomy 31:10). On that last day, as the trumpet sounds, the *ekklesia* will be gathered before God as He moves among us. What an exciting prospect to be in that gathering. It is the climax of the word (and concept) of *ekklesia*, our ultimate destination.

I hope you can now see how the word *ekklesia* has been mistranslated and misused in the last 2000 years. It was never intended to denote a building or a hierarchical system. It was always meant to signify the assembly of God’s people when even “two or three are gathered in my name, there am I with them” (Matthew 18:20). We don’t need a huge crowd to meet as an *ekklesia;* even two or three will do! We can be confident of our understanding of this amazing word—Jesus did not say “I will build my “church”” or “I will build my synagogue”, But “I will build my *ekklesia*” (Matthew 16;18).

The significance of this little ancient word is huge. Jesus never asked us to form hierarchical organizations and to separate out the clergy from the laity, nor to build buildings—even if we said it was all in His name and to His glory. It is so much simpler than that. Just meet with a few like-minded people at home or a café or on the beach or anywhere. Because Jesus promises he will be there. How awesome is that?

REFLECTIONS

Do you go to church? Are there ways of practicing your Christianity other than going to church?

Other than a church building, are there other locations we can "do church"?

Do you belong to the Christian faith or to a Christian Church? Can you belong to both?

Can you be a proponent of Methodism, Anglicanism or other denomination and believe in the unity of the ekklesia?

Does your church focus on acquiring the resources needed to run the organization, thereby making the running of the church an end *in itself? Or does it focus on being the* means *to introduce you to an encounter with God?*

5

THE TEMPLE DISMANTLED

In this short book, we are looking at the elements that we have come to think of as integral to formal Christianity—and have begun to question them! The church building is one of those elements. But how did we come to place so much importance on this strange edifice? Let us explore.

In pre-history, religions emerged all over the world, developing their specific rituals and customs. A feature of many of these religions, including those around the Mediterranean, was the building of temples as places where their rituals could be performed. The Greeks and the Romans were particularly good at building extravagant temples to various gods. Sacrifices and other rituals were offered in them. There were even temples with shrine prostitutes where devotees could be united with the gods.

It is possible to see the foreshadowing of a temple in the garden of Eden as the place where God walked and communed with Adam and Eve. Prior to an actual construction, an image of the Jewish temple also emerged later in Genesis as an altar, presumably outside in the fresh air and was built for offering sacrifices to Jehovah (Genesis 8:20). Later, around 1350-1230BC, God told Moses to build the tabernacle in the desert, giving him very precise instructions about how to build it and its contents. This was a sort of temple-on-the-go and could be picked up and carried to the next place God led the Israelites to in the wilderness. The Holy Place and the Holy of Holies were by now under a tent covering, and, like the Garden of Eden, God's presence was there.

Around 1300BC, the Israelites took the tabernacle containing the ark across the Jordan River and laid it to rest at Shiloh. Here it remained for a long time. King David eventually moved the tabernacle and the ark to Jerusalem around 1000BC.

Around 970-930BC, King David's son and heir, Solomon, built the first stone temple which looked a lot like the tabernacle in form and function. This was known as the First Temple. However, it became a target for envious rulers of the region, and the temple was plundered eight times up until 587BC when Nebuchadnezzar finally destroyed Jerusalem and the temple (2 Kings 19:1). The Israelites were exiled to Babylon but were able to return after 70 years. They rebuilt the temple which became known as the Second Temple. Between 20BC and 9AD, Herod the Great renovated the Second Temple, the one Jesus would have seen. Soon after this, the Romans were so angered by the Jewish uprising against them that they completely sacked and destroyed the temple in 70AD.

The sacking by Rome in 70AD was of enormous significance to both Jew and Christian. For the Jew, it signified the end to temple worship and animal sacrifice and initiated the dispersal of the people out of the Promised Land (the diaspora). Likewise, it marked the persecution and scattering of the early Christians to other parts of the Roman Empire including east toward India and west toward Asia Minor (modern-day Turkey), Greece and Rome (Acts 8:1). Later, John had a vision on the island of Patmos, seeing a new heaven and a new earth. Looking at the New Jerusalem, he commented, "I did not see a temple in the city, because the Lord God Almighty and the lamb are its temple." (Revelation 21:22).[3]

---

[3] In the spirit of honesty, there is also a quote from Revelation 11:19 that says: "Then God's temple in heaven was opened, and within the temple was seen the ark of the covenant." The Greek word for temple (naos) is the same as used in 21:22. We do not know where God's heaven is, but it does not sound as if it is in the New Jerusalem. It is in the "Ouranos" from whence the New Jerusalem descends. I believe that heaven (Ouranos) or paradise is like the antechamber of the New Jerusalem. I think God will sit on his throne in His heaven until Judgment Day when the New Heaven and the New Earth will come down from the Ouranos and God will no longer need a temple.

John's remark takes us right back to Eden. At last, we are again free to roam the garden and commune with God as He strolls with us. On the day of crucifixion, the curtain in the temple was torn from top to bottom, allowing all to have direct access to the Father (Matthew 27:51), all thanks to Jesus' sacrificial death on the cross. Christians now have no need of a building to approach God.

Paul describes how believers met in private homes during the first century AD (Romans 16:3-5)[4]. The bible provides no evidence of any Christian group meeting in a dedicated building after that. Indeed, we have no evidence that dedicated buildings were used by Christians until Emperor Constantine declared Christianity to be the official religion of the Roman Empire. He then encouraged Christians to meet in the former pagan temples for worship. Wow. We discuss what happened next in the Chapter 11 on the Reformation.

The use of Romanesque temples/churches continues to this day. It can be seen in the wonderful and glorious architecture of the cathedrals of Europe. As Christianity spread, every community felt the need for a church building to meet in. There was always a sanctum at one end where the altar was positioned—very similar to the tabernacle and temples. Master craftsmen built the very best buildings of the time, resulting in wonderful cathedrals with revolutionary architecture, all to the glory of God. Were they wrong to return to the temple model?

To be darkly cynical, the building of such grand places of worship DID have other motives. In Britain, the largely Celtic form of Christianity was flourishing until the Norman invasion of 1066AD. The Normans brought conquest, subjugation, and the Roman church with them. Building cathedrals and castles was all part of the statement, "We are strong, and we intend to stay. Get used to it!" Similar motives in other parts of Christendom were at work. As far east as Byzantium, building programs proclaimed the power and authority of the Roman rulers.

[4] See the chapter on House Churches for a wider discussion.

I have met priests and vicars who have been assigned a parish that has a church that is several hundred years old. I am certain that these facilities are probably wonderful buildings and full of history, but the incumbent finds herself/himself spending all her/his time and energy trying to raise money to repair the roof that is in danger of falling in and ruining the entire building. People do not have the faith to believe God for the resources they need for His ministry. Even the resources that are available may not be used for the Kingdom. We are spending precious resources on buildings and other requirements of the organized church. What a waste.

Don't get me wrong: I love these heritage buildings. Yes, they should be preserved for posterity, but not at the expense of God's work. One cannot but respect the builders of the great churches and cathedrals, who were likely dedicated Christians wanting to build something that glorified God. And when you hear a cathedral choir sing evensong in one of these buildings, you are certainly transported to heavenly places.

Immediately after Pentecost, the new converts met in the arcade round the temple. They met in ever-increasing numbers "Every day they met together in the temple courts" (Acts 2:46). They also met in homes to break bread. Meeting in the temple courts was a mass gathering, and I can imagine the excitement as people gathered in their thousands. I have taken part in a worship service in a huge auditorium with 30,000 other Christians, and the atmosphere is amazing. One can imagine the space above the people being filled with angels. There are clearly moments where it is appropriate for large numbers of Christians to gather other than in private homes. A Billy Graham crusade held in a football stadium presents another good example.

We seem to have been determined to reinvent the temple. Perhaps it is getting in the way of the true *ekklesia* and needs to be dismantled.

REFLECTIONS

Do we need churches and cathedrals as places to worship God? Are these buildings using up resources incorrectly and are they actually inappropriate, being reminiscent of pagan temples?

Did God want to stop animal sacrifice AND temple worship at the cross?

Why did God ask Moses to build the tabernacle and Solomon to build the temple? And why did he ask Ezra and Nehemiah to repair it on their return from exile, when God knew it was soon going to be destroyed?

Why did God allow the temple to be sacked so conclusively? Was He wanting to put an end to building and using such places?

Apart from the use of the temple courts immediately after Pentecost, why is there no mention of temples in the New Testament? Does the model for fellowship provided by the New Testament in the post-Jesus era mention meeting in any building other than private homes?

6

THE ORDAINED PRIESTHOOD

Recognizing the reality that we are not a physical church but a gathering of faithful people, let us now turn to examining those who populate the *ekklesia*. Considering the previous chapter on dismantling the temple, we seem to have queered the pitch somewhat for the ordained priest who now has no facility to amplify his preaching! Let us explore.

Christianity was not the first faith to appoint priests. While we were hunter-gatherers (many moons ago!), we were too focused on survival to support specialized members of the tribe. But once humans became settled in cities, it became possible for individuals to undertake specialized roles. This would have included potters and other artisan trades as well as priests. A priest emerged as a person authorized to perform the sacred rituals of a religion, especially as a mediator between humans and the gods. He also had the authority or power to administer religious rites; in particular, the rites of sacrifice to deities. They generally dressed differently from the general population to emphasize their position, authority, and power. They would probably have been paid by the community, or at least supported by them.

Within the Old Testament, God ordained an Israelite priesthood with Aaron as the chief priest, under whom was a cadre of priests who had duties to perform in the tabernacle—later to become the temple. The Aaronic priests stood between the people and God, offering sacrifices on behalf of the people for sins committed.

But God did not limit the priesthood to Aaronic priestly appointments. He said: "Now therefore, if you will indeed obey my voice and keep my covenant, you shall be my treasured possession among all peoples, for all the earth is mine; and you shall be to me *a kingdom of priests* and a holy nation." (Exodus 19:5–6). Isaiah takes up this theme in Chapter 61: "The Spirit of the Sovereign Lord is on me...And you will be called priests of the Lord, you will be named ministers of our God."

We must wait until the New Testament to see the next step, this time taken by Jesus. In Luke 4:16-21, Jesus stood up in the synagogue and reminded everyone what Isaiah had said. Jesus read Isaiah's passage out loud and said, "Today this scripture is fulfilled in your hearing."

On the afternoon of Jesus' crucifixion, the curtain hiding the Holy of Holies was torn from top to bottom, allowing direct access for all believers into the presence of God (Matthew 27:51). The new promise was implemented while the old temple order was abolished (although the old order staggered on until the sacking of the temple in 70AD).

By the time of Jesus, the Aaronic priesthood had already gone off the rails. Jesus warns in Matthew 23:

> Then Jesus said to the crowds and to his disciples: "The teachers of the law and the Pharisees sit in Moses' seat. So, you must be careful to do everything they tell you. But do not do what they do, for they do not practice what they preach. They tie up heavy, cumbersome loads and put them on other people's shoulders, but they themselves are not willing to lift a finger to move them. Everything they do is done for people to see: they make their phylacteries wide and the tassels on their garments long; they love the place of honour at banquets and the most important seats in the synagogues; they love to be greeted with respect in the marketplaces and to be called 'Rabbi' by others. But you are not to be called 'Rabbi,' for you have one Teacher, and you are all brothers. And do not call anyone on earth 'father,' for you have one Father, and he is in heaven. Nor

> are you to be called instructors, for you have one Instructor, the Messiah. The greatest among you will be your servant. For those who exalt themselves will be humbled, and those who humble themselves will be exalted."

In the New Testament, the Aaronic priesthood was abolished at the cross. There are no popes, bishops, or priests to rule over the church. Jesus Christ is our High Priest, not following the Aaronic priesthood, but in the order of Melchizedek (Hebrews 3:1; 4:14-15; 5:5; 8:1; 9:11), and all true Christians make up a spiritual priesthood. Peter declares: "But you are a chosen people, a royal priesthood, a holy nation, a people belonging to God." (I Peter 2:5). By His death, Jesus Christ has sanctified (made holy) all Christians who believe in Him (Hebrews 10:10-11).

And the writer of Revelation says: "To him who loves us and has freed us from sin by his blood and has made us (believers) to be a kingdom and priests to serve his God and Father" (Revelation 1:5-6). Finally in Revelation, twenty-four Elders sang to Jesus: "You have made them (believers) to be a kingdom and priests to serve God, and they will reign on the earth." (Revelation 5:10)

THOSE IN THE DENOMINATIONAL ORDAINED PRIESTHOOD

We need some discussion about who exactly is an ordained priest today (in contrast to all believers who are royal priests through faith in Jesus). There appears to be a spectrum, a continuum that makes it hard to draw a definite line. At one extreme is the Catholic or Orthodox priest who wears a collar and black robes—no mistaking him as an ordained priest. At the other extreme is the laid-back leader of an informal home church who is looked to by others in the group for order and leadership. They do not call themselves a pastor, vicar, or priest, but their function is to bring order into the group (an expression of the *ekklesia*). There is every shade of leadership between these two extremes, and it is not my call to make a judgment about where a given individual sits on the spectrum. You will know by the fruits of their lives (Galatians 5) which side of the line they fall. Some Protestant church systems demand full ordination to appoint an individual as a priest. Others demand only evidence of biblical training before appointment. But if they are operating as a priest within a religious system, whatever it is called, they are likely perpetuating the clergy-laity divide.

Are those individuals wrong who are currently or have been in a denominational priesthood? If that is where God has placed someone, of course it is not wrong. There have been wonderful, ordained men and women of faith throughout the ages who have been godly, doing what God wanted them to do. Often persons who felt the call of God on their lives saw only limited options to express that calling. It would have been natural for them to look to the conventional priesthood for that fulfillment. Sadly, the idea of entering the priesthood was also sometimes seen as a good career move. Second sons were often expected to enter the priesthood, regardless of calling. Indeed, for some, it was a career promising riches and power. But it does not alter my premise that there can be only one high priest, Jesus, and all other believers are members of the royal priesthood.

> "As Christ is the only mediator between God and man, any usurping of His priesthood can only be described as the spirit of anti-Christ. And yet that is exactly what happened as the concept of *official power* grew in the church. A priesthood developed, with abuses down through history that defy imagination" (*David Orton, 2019*).

REFLECTIONS

The scriptures I have quoted in this chapter are the basis of the understanding of the "Priesthood of all believers." If you accept the scriptures I have quoted above, there are some serious questions to answer about the ordained priesthood today.

Did the first century church have specially designated priests/clergy, or was everyone equal?

Why do priests dress differently from the wider population? Is it to emphasize their power and authority, perpetuating the Old Testament idea that there is a clergy and a laity?

What functions can an ordained priest perform that ordinary Christians cannot? If I am already a royal priest, can I not also share bread and wine at communion with other believers? Can I not pray for others? Can I not baptize?[5]

What is the value of denominational ordination when a specific denomination declares an individual to be "an ordained priest"? Are they not already royal priests?

Can a homosexual or transgender person be ordained? I think that is a wrong question—the real question is can a homosexual or transgender person be a believing, practicing Christian? If you believe that they cannot *be a true believer while in that state, then of course they are not yet royal priests. If you believe that such a person* can *be a practicing Christian, they are already a royal priest. Either way, they should not or do not need to be "ordained"!*

What effect does celibacy[6] *have on homosexual behaviour and pedophilia in the ordained priesthood? (If all believers are royal priests, enforced celibacy for priests would wipe out Christianity in a generation!)*

Does having an ordained priest appointed over a congregation inhibit the laity from becoming mature Christians who can express their giftings fully?

[5] I have married couples before God, but in most countries, marriage must be carried out by an authorised celebrant, otherwise it is not legal. Some couples choose to be married before God first and then submit to the authorised celebrant later to make the marriage legal.

[6] Celibacy is not required anywhere in the scriptures. Paul was celibate but made it clear that if you burn with passion, you had better get married!

Perhaps there are those who could preach, teach, or evangelize but do not feel empowered to do so while there is a person paid to do all that.

As all believers are royal priests, should we all get paid, or should none of us get paid?

Would it ruin God's plan for our redemption if there were no ordained priests?

7

PAGAN TRADITIONS

Christianity did not destroy paganism, it adopted it.[7]

Several elements of today's Christianity are indispensable in the minds of many people. Of course, we go to church on Sunday. Yes, the vicar will preach a sermon after the choir has sung an anthem. And so on. How did these practices and traditions emerge and where did they come from? Are they in the scriptures? In fact, most of the traditions came from the adoption of Christianity by the Roman Empire.

7.1 PAGAN CHRISTIANITY

In Chapter 11 on the Reformation, we will deal with the historical events surrounding how the *ekklesia* was radically changed by Emperor Constantine in 315AD. The process he began resulted in the wholesale adoption of many pagan practices into the Christian church. Because the Empire had been firmly pagan until then, worshipping many gods (including the emperor himself), Constantine needed to make the transition as acceptable as possible for the pagans who were, after all, in the majority. He did this by simply superimposing Christian festivals and practices onto existing pagan ones. You may be surprised at how many elements of present-day Christianity have pagan origins.

[7] Will Durant. Twentieth Century historian.

The church building. We discuss the pagan origins of the church building in the chapter on The Temple.

The sermon. What church service would be complete without a sermon? Are you kidding? There can't be a churchgoer alive who has not suffered through torture, longing for the vicar to stop talking. Is God edified by a good sermon? Probably not! Are the people edified by a good sermon? Probably not. Anyone who has studied the transfer of knowledge knows that little if any information is transferred by one person speaking and a lot of others listening passively. Visual aids increase learning, but best of all is interaction and practical application. The sermon is delivered to a passive audience, ignoring the basic understanding of the transfer of knowledge.

So where did the sermon come from? It clearly was not around in Jesus' time. Although he taught, he delivered *impromptu* lessons with easy-to-understand applications (parables). There was always audience participation. His teaching was not "every Sabbath at 9am in the synagogue." The early church meetings in homes certainly did not have sermons. The heritage is from the Greek sophists who took public speaking to dizzy heights and were revered for it.

By the fourth century the sermon was part of Christian gatherings. It had a resurgence again in the worship service at the time of Luther. Does it matter? It makes the preacher a virtuoso performer, it offers practical advice rather than presenting the gospel (listen to Joyce Meyer or Joel Osteen as examples), it perpetuates the clergy/laity divide, and it enforces audience passivity.

"Neither homilies (sermons) nor homiletics (the art of sermonising) has a Christian origin. They were stolen from the Pagan. A polluted stream made its entrance into the Christian faith and muddied the waters. And that stream flows just as it did in the fourth century."[8]

---

[8] The sermon: Protestantism's sacred cow. In Pagan Christianity? Viola F and Barna G. Tyndale 2002.

The pulpit. The equivalent of a pulpit was used in the pre-Christian era in the Jewish synagogue and pagan temples. As the early Christians met in places other than churches or temples, the pulpit clearly did not serve as a feature at this time. Only after Christians moved into buildings in the fourth century was a place required for the bishop to sit (the bishop's throne) and, later, to provide a place to preach from (the ambo or platform, later to be enlarged to a pulpit in the manner of the pagan temple).

Robes. Special robes have always distinguished clergy from laity. But in the first three centuries, Christians met so informally that there were no special robes because there were no clergy. Clergy did not dress differently from common people until the coming of Constantine. The white robes of the Roman civil authority were adopted but gradually more ornate vestments evolved. The Reformation replaced the elaborate dress of the Catholic priest with the sombre black of the cleric. "A specially attired clergy is an affront to the spiritual principles that govern the House of God. It strikes at the heart of the church by separating God's people into two classes: professional and non-professional."[9]

Music. This is a tricky one. Choirs, singing, processing and special robes were all part of the pre-Christian Roman Pagan traditions. In that sense, church music has some pagan origins. But the Old Testament describes joyful singing, praising with the harp and lyre, and with trumpets in the temple. If you have ever attended a Jewish wedding, you will know just what a joyful sound the guests can make! David played and sang to King Saul. We can equally say, then, that church music has some Jewish origins. But the first century Christians would have had no instruments to aid their singing. Everyone was instructed to bring a song. The praise and worship would have been spontaneous. Today in many larger churches, the musical component of the service

---

[9] Pagan Christianity. Viola F and Barna G. pp154.

will be carefully integrated with the readings and teachings. It will not be brought spontaneously by the congregation but will be pre-planned. The choir will be dressed in clergy-like robes and will sit in special seats near the altar. This emphasizes the clergy-laity divide. The ordinary church member sitting in the pew is passive, standing to sing what he/she is told to sing when the right part of the service is reached. I acknowledge that many non-denominational churches are much more relaxed than that and I would not presume to judge them on that basis. My personal dismay is when worship leaders become the focus of attention (even adoration) at the front of the people and the service becomes a rock concert with instruments and voices amplified to eardrum-crushing levels. Did I miss something? Is the praise better if it is louder? "This is the one I esteem: he who is humble and contrite in spirit, and trembles at my word." (Isaiah 66:2).

There is, in my opinion, an undoubted place for sacred music, but how that fits into the Christian faith is not obvious.

Bells. The sound of church bells has been a familiar sound associated by Christians with joyful events such as baptism, weddings or simply a call to Sunday worship. Catholic mass uses the bell in the service. The idea that the sound of bells ringing has spiritual value is thought to have originated with ancient winter celebrations in which bells were rung to drive out evil spirits. Some churches still refer to the so-called apotropaic power (supposed power to avert evil influences or bad luck) of bells in their descriptions of sanctus bells.

Incense. The use of incense in the ancient world was common, especially in religious rites where it was used to keep demons away. Herodotus, the Greek historian, recorded that it was popular among the Assyrians, Babylonians, and Egyptians. Jews also used it in thanksgiving offerings (Numbers 7:14).[10] God instructs Moses to build an altar and burn

---

[10] Why do priests use incense? Fr William Saunders. https://www.catholiceducation.org/en/culture/catholic-contributions/why-do-priests-use-incense.html

"fragrant incense for the Holy Place" (Exodus 31:11). We can assume from this that the origin of its use was pagan, but it became acceptable to God as it represented the prayers of the faithful, "And when he had taken the scroll, the four living creatures and the twenty-four elders fell down before the Lamb, each holding a harp, and golden bowls full of incense, which are the prayers of the saints (Revelation 5:8).

7.2 CHRISTIAN FESTIVALS

For hundreds of years, Christians have enjoyed various festivals and traditions throughout the seasons. But it may come as a surprise that few are of biblically based Christian origins. Let us consider some of the major festivals that we enjoy so much.

Lent is a period when we are meant to fast, lasting for approximately six weeks leading up to Easter Sunday. It runs from Ash Wednesday to Maundy Thursday (Holy Thursday) morning or to Easter Eve. In the past, Christians who had committed grave faults performed public penance. On Ash Wednesday, the bishop blessed the hair shirts which they were to wear during the forty days of penance and sprinkled over them ashes made from the palms from the previous year. Then, while the faithful recited the Seven Penitential Psalms, the penitents were turned out of the church because of their sins -- just as Adam, the first man, was turned out of paradise because of his disobedience. The penitents did not enter the church again until Maundy Thursday after having won reconciliation by the toil of forty days' penance and sacramental absolution.

Jesus spent 40 days fasting in the desert. But Jesus did not fast 40 days BEFORE Passover/Easter; rather, he fasted AFTER his baptism. Thus, Lent may have biblical overtones, but it does not represent a specific event in the life of Jesus before his crucifixion, nor is it mentioned in scriptures.

Good Friday wasn't Good Friday, it was Good Wednesday! For Jesus to have been in the tomb three days and have risen on the Sunday, he would have had to be buried before 6pm on the Wednesday. This does not alter the validity of setting aside a day to remember the sacrifice Jesus made on the cross for our redemption, but it is worth noting that calling it Good *Friday* is inaccurate!

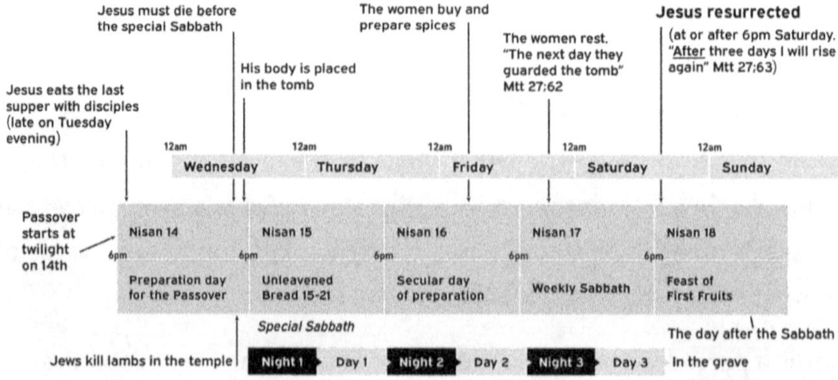

Easter Sunday commemorates the day Jesus rose from the dead—definitely scriptural! It was determined by the church fathers that Easter should coincide with the Jewish feast of Passover, an eminently sensible decision as Jesus was crucified on Passover.

Passover represents Israel's deliverance out of Egyptian bondage and the preparation for moving into a new life in the promised land. The festival is loaded with symbolism for the Jew as it involves eating unleavened bread (the absence of sin) and the flesh of a male yearling lamb, without blemish, as a burnt offering to the Lord. The lamb's shed blood had to be smeared over the door post to protect the family. Sadly, much of that symbolism is lost in the Christian festival of Easter.

However, the very name of "Easter" is Pagan, referencing the goddess Ishtar, who was the goddess of springtime and fertility. Her symbols include rabbits, Maypoles (umbilical cord), and eggs—"Oestrus".

Advent anticipates the coming of the Messiah. It is four weeks prior to Christmas. While appropriate to recognize that anticipation, there is nothing in the Bible that suggests this should be performed as a festival.

FESTIVAL	PURPOSE	ORIGIN
Shrove Tuesday	Use up rich food before Lent	Pagan
Ash Wednesday	Start of Lent and penance	Barely biblical
Lent	40 days of fasting leading to Easter	Barely biblical
Maundy Thursday	Jesus washing feet, alms giving	Barely biblical
Good Friday	Jesus crucified	Biblical
Easter Day	Jesus risen, Spring festival	Biblical/Jewish/Pagan
Ascension Day	Jesus' ascension to heaven	Biblical
Whitsun	Pentecost, giving of the law and HS	Biblical/Jewish
Autumn Festival	Celebrate the harvest	Jewish/Pagan
Halloween	Festival of the dead	Pagan
All Saints Day	Celebrates those who have attained sainthood	Not biblical
Advent	Anticipates the coming of Christ	Not biblical
Winter Solstice	Turning point of winter	Pagan
Christmas Eve	Night before Christmas	Not biblical
Christmas Day	Birth of Christ, Winter festival	Biblical and Pagan
Boxing Day	Giving of gifts to servants	Not biblical
12 days of Christmas	12 days of Christmas celebration	Pagan
Hogmanay	Scottish New Year	Pagan
Yuletide	Midwinter festival—Germanic	Pagan
Epiphany	Realisation that Jesus is Christ	Barely biblical

The above table reveals that our Christian calendar that we take for granted is littered with inaccuracies and pagan practices. At least Ascension Day and Whit Sunday are biblical. Not only do we celebrate festivals of pagan origin, but we dilute and even lose the biblical significance by rampant commercialism of those few festivals we can justify.

Christmas Day is probably the most celebrated festival globally and commemorates the birth of Jesus—again very scriptural. But the date chosen coincides with the festival of the winter solstice and the beginning of the new year—Pagan. The choice for this date was not helped by a lack of precision in the Bible as to when exactly Jesus was born. So, to cause as little disruption as possible during the change-over from pagan to Christian religion in the Roman world, a date was chosen that was already in use for the winter festival.

My best guess about the actual date of Jesus' birth would be Nissan 1 (new moon) in 6BC. That would have been when the shepherds were out in the fields for the lambing season (April). But that discussion is for another book!

An epiphany is an experience of sudden and striking realization. In this context, it is a realization that Christ is the son of God. Western churches generally celebrate the Visit of the Magi as the revelation of the birth of Christ and commemorate the Feast of the Epiphany on January 6. In terms of accuracy, one should point out that the wise men arrived about two years after his birth!

7.3 JEWISH ORIGINS

Christianity is built on Judaism and holds Jesus, a Jew, as the Son of God. Therefore, it is, in my opinion, an easy transition to make from Passover to Easter. And the transition from breaking the bread at the start of the Sabbath to Holy Communion is honouring to its roots. However, it becomes a difficult issue when we consider Easter bunnies, chocolate eggs and the Maypole, harking back not to Judaism but to Ishtar, the pagan goddess of fertility.

7.4 NON-BIBLICAL PRACTICES

It would be wrong to condemn every practice in today's church. One cannot generalize—some practices have emerged from a pagan past while others have purer origins. Here are some mixed examples:

Praying to Mary. I deal with the inappropriateness and Pagan origins of this practice in the chapter on the Roman Catholic Church.

Lent. Fasting for forty days before celebrating Easter sounds a positive exercise, as is fasting for shorter periods. Jesus encourages fasting when he says that some unclean spirits cannot be shifted without fasting. He did fast for forty days after his baptism. If the Lent fasting brings individuals into a closer communion with God, I heartily commend it. My only proviso is that it is not a requirement laid out in scripture—Jesus did not fast for forty days before his crucifixion.

Maundy Thursday. Tradition dictates that alms are given to the poor on Maundy Thursday. Again, one cannot fault the action, only to comment that it is not something mentioned in scriptures that should be limited to the day before crucifixion.

First communion on Whit Sunday. There is no direct link between Pentecost (when the law and the Holy Spirit were given) and first communion. But I see nothing amiss with the practice if that is a local tradition.

The bishop's crook. This rod with the hooked end is a quintessential symbol of the modern bishop. It is symbolic of his/her shepherding role and resonates with the teachings of Jesus who proclaimed he was the Good Shepherd. But Jesus did not carry a crook, nor did he wear a mitre or ornate robes. These accoutrements of the bishop were always designed to emphasize his lofty status not just above the laity, but above his fellow clergy.

Gold and silver altar vessels. It is hard to find fault with the principle of giving God the best. And that is what the Israelites did in temple worship. I am sure the vessels they used were of the best silver and gold they could find. But the first century Christians would not have had access to such riches. When they broke bread and took the wine of Communion, they would have used whatever vessels were to hand. But if the gold and silver or the Leonardo altarpiece were purchased with funds that could have gone to the poor, that may put a different light on it.

7.5 TO CELEBRATE OR NOT?

For many Christians, celebrating the festivals (particularly Christmas) is the very essence of Christianity. They would complain bitterly at any suggestion of change. Should we encourage believers to avoid festivals with Pagan origins? Should we reconsider how we celebrate the birth of Christ and his resurrection?

Maybe it is wrong to celebrate any festival if it has a pagan origin. My personal belief is that if you know an event is of pagan roots, you also know that it is not pure and is tainted. I would not enjoy that event. But if you understand its roots and can celebrate to the Lord on that day, maybe that is OK. A personal choice. A clear exception I would personally make is the celebration of Halloween that is not only pagan, but extremely dark. It is wrong at so many levels for Christian families to celebrate it and to encourage their children to take part. No, it is not simply fun with a sugar rush.

There have been practices that have emerged during the last 2000 years that are neither pagan nor Jewish in origin, and neither are they mentioned in the Bible. The chances are that these practices emerged out of incorrect theology. Yes, in my opinion, they should be avoided.

REFLECTIONS

So many festivals and practices of Catholic and Protestant church life are steeped in paganism. Does it matter? Should we scrap the lot? Is it compromise to continue with them?

Is the acid test whether festivals and activities are endorsed in the New Testament? What other criteria for evaluating them could we use?

Should we use music and song to worship our Maker? How can we make it relevant to our culture?

8

ELDERS, BISHOPS, AND DEACONS

Another title for this chapter might equally have been "Servant Leaders". But who are these servant leaders?

We have discussed in Chapter 6 the importance of understanding that all believers are royal priests. We also know that each believer/royal priest is endowed with at least one spiritual gift for the edification of the body of Christ. As well, the five-fold ministry identifies five functions of those willing to serve in ministry.

But if everyone is equal before the Lord, who leads? Well, there is one clear boss—Jesus is the high priest: "And God placed all things under his feet and appointed him to be head over everything." (Ephesians 1:22).

But after that, who are the leaders? The answer is everyone and no one! Every one of us is responsible for our own behaviour. We cannot look to others such as paid staff to do what we should be doing. And no one can claim his/her action was the responsibility of others.

But God's house is a house of order. And there are some things that need to be achieved corporately. The Bible has the answer! No single person is in charge. But certain persons are appointed to lead in accomplishing certain tasks so that there should be order and so that no one should fall through the cracks.

God's advice to Moses was to "Appoint seventy elders who will help carry the burden of the people so that you will not have to carry it alone." (Numbers 11:16). The word "elders" in the Septuagint is *presbuteros*, indicating that the idea of appointing respected members of the community to run affairs was well established by the time of the Jewish exodus from Egypt. Later, the Jews were not allowed to rule when they were taken over by the Greeks then by the Romans, but they were allowed to govern their own spiritual affairs with the Sanhedrin—a council of elders. In Matthew 26:3, the chief priests and elders (*presbuteros*) plotted to kill Jesus. They had no civil authority but exercised their influence over the spiritual care of the people. In this instance, they went far beyond their remit by influencing the political outcome to kill Jesus.

In alignment with the Jewish tradition, Paul identified two types of overseers or leaders for the church: elders (or bishops) and deacons. The elders were appointed as servant leaders, not to control. They were appointed to provide spiritual care of and to exercise oversight over the people, and they managed public affairs.

GREEK WORD	TRANSLITERATION	MEANING	REFERENCE
πρεσβυτερος	presbuteros	Elder	Titus 1:5 Vine 4245
διακονος	diakonos	Deacon, servant, one who executes the orders of another	1Tim 3:8 Vine 1249
επισκοπος	episkopos	skopos = watch out for, pay attention to, bishop	1Tim 3:1 Vine 1985

Paul says that if anyone desires to be an overseer *(episkopos)*, he desires a noble task (1Timothy 3;1). He uses the Greek word *episkopos* which can be translated as overseer, elder or bishop. In verse 4, he suggests that taking care of God's church is not so different from managing a family! It is hard to see how Paul distinguishes between *presbuteros* and *episkopos*—presumably the terms are interchangeable. Paul focuses on the *quality and character* of the elder rather than a specific job description. He does not suggest that elders *cannot* or do not teach, preach, or evangelize, and neither does he suggest that the elders *should* undertake these tasks.

Paul describes a second cadre, the helpers of the elders called deacons (1Timothy 3:8). The word he uses is *diakonos* which means "a servant" or "one who executes the command of another". The other Greek word used is *hyperetes,* which literally means "the under-rower" or the subordinate who is doing the rowing of a boat. Thus, a deacon works for both God and man in service. Just as Jesus was a servant to both God and man, so should all believers be.

During the first century when these terms were being applied to Christians, there were no denominations. Each town or city containing groups of Christians needed oversight. Thus, the appointment of elders and deacons would have been for oversight of the entire town or city. We discuss the meaning of *ekklesia* elsewhere, but the appointment of elders and deacons is intended for oversight of the entire community of believers in each city or town (the *ekklesia*).

These roles were quite difficult to execute as they did not come with "seniority" over the other Christians. That is why Paul focuses on *character* and stipulates the elders must be mature believers—they had to function as servant-leaders. They were not given special robes, did not undertake ceremonial duties, were not paid, but needed to earn the respect of those whom they served. In summary, then, the appointment of elders and deacons was for each geographical area where there were Christians, probably not for each small group of believers.

We should not be in a hurry to be elders. If God has not called us, we should not seek such an appointment. Even more so, if we are elders, God requires a high standard. He does not appreciate leaders who lead people the wrong way. Isaiah puts it like this: "The Lord enters into judgment against the elders and the leaders of his people; 'It is you who have ruined my vineyard; the plunder from the poor is in your houses.'" (Isaiah 3:14). (See also Chapter 13 on False Teachers).

There is another group of individuals who should be mentioned—the Church Fathers. These were men whose faith shone through and whose wisdom was clear to see. They had a tremendous influence on the emerging churches all over the known world. Such men transcend the categories offered by Paul (above) and were instrumental in steering Christianity through the centuries. The early Fathers such as Clement, Ignatius, and Polycarp were theologians who lived in the 1st and 2nd centuries AD, who are believed to have personally known some of the Twelve Apostles, or to have been significantly influenced by them. Their writings, though popular in Early Christianity, were ultimately not included in the canon of the New Testament once it reached its final form, however.

There is room for misunderstanding between the appointment of the two categories of servant leaders (elders and deacons) and the acceptance that every Christian is a royal priest. Sadly, this was exploited in the second century when ambitious men saw a chance to take control. Bishops emerged who many times assumed inappropriate power and authority. The issue of authority has been at the root of the division between clergy and laity for two millennia, and tragically has caused enormous damage to the faith. THERE IS NO LAITY! THERE IS ONLY ONE PRIESTHOOD AND ONLY ONE HIGH PRIEST—Jesus.

There is a constant tension between the charismatic and the institution. In Acts, the focus is initially very much on the charismatic, but before long the need for structure and order forced its way through with the appearance of bishops/elders and deacons. Fallen humanity gains comfort from order in the form of institutions, in the case of the church, at the expense of the charismatic. The challenge is to avoid the tendency to form institutions, but to keep our eyes on Jesus. The Church He came to create is a Holy Spirit-filled community that is instructed to fill every part of the world with His fullness. Alas, we have been determined to perpetuate the religious system. It has seemed safer that way. This false system must be dismantled while maintaining God-ordained servant-leaders.

REFLECTIONS

What authority do elders and deacons exercise?

Why does the Bible describe the required character *for servant leaders, but not* job descriptions?

Should elders and deacons have responsibilities for running the church? Or should it be left to the priest, vicar, or pastor to run everything?

Does the priest/vicar/minister outrank the elders?

Is it a positive contribution to the ekklesia *to have bishops/elders and deacons appointed?*

9

THE FIVEFOLD MINISTRY AND THE GIFTS

In the previous chapter, I have discussed how elders and deacons are invaluable servant-leaders. While not everyone is called to be an elder or deacon, we are all called to proclaim the gospel. The most natural next step after we accept Jesus as our Saviour is the desire to further His kingdom on Earth through a life of service and witness. God does not cast us out into the community and tell us just to get on with it. He equips us before He sends us into battle. Through His grace toward each of us individually, this equipping is achieved by the gifts He endows us with. Not everyone receives the same gifts. God also calls certain individuals to specific ministries. Regardless of gifting and regardless of ministry calling, we are all the same status—royal priests under one High Priest.

THE GIFTS

Every believer is endowed with at least one spiritual gift. There are several lists in the New Testament that categorize the possible gifts, but the lists are not exhaustive. We will look at the various gifts and hopefully understand their purpose. The gifts must be used in love and are not for the recipient's aggrandizement. They are for building the *ekklesia*.

Paul sums the gifts up as follows: "Now about spiritual gifts, brothers, I do not want you to be ignorant. There are different kinds of *gifts*, but the same Spirit. There are different kinds of *service*, but the same Lord. There are different kinds of *working* but the same God works all of them in all men" (1 Corinthians 12).

Paul explains our interdependence: "Just as each of us has one body with many members, and those members do not all have the same function, so in Christ we who are many form one body, and each member belongs to all the others. We have different gifts, according to the grace given us". (Romans 12:4).

This table lists gifts mentioned in five locations in the Bible:

ISAIAH 11:2*	1CORINTHIANS 12 VS7-11	1CORINTHIANS 12 VS 27-31	ROMANS 12	1PETER 4
Wisdom	Wisdom	Apostle		
Under-standing	Distinguishing spirits		Mercy	
Counsel	Faith	Leadership		
Power	Miraculous powers	Worker of miracles		
Knowledge	Knowledge	Teacher	Teach	
Fear of the Lord	Prophecy	Prophet	Prophecy	Speak
*These are the fruits of the Messiah predicted by Isaiah	Healings	Healing		
	Tongues	Tongues		
	Interpret tongues	Helping others	Serve	Serve
		Administration	Encourage	
			Give/share	
			Hospitality	Hospitality

In three separate passages Paul then describe how the essential ingredient to accompany any and every of the gifts is love:

> And now I will show you the most excellent way. If I speak in tongues of men and of angels, but have no love, I am only a resounding gong or a clanging cymbal. If I have the gift of prophecy and can fathom all mysteries and all knowledge, and if I have faith that can move mountains, but have not love, I am nothing. If I give all I possess to

> the poor and surrender my body to the flames, but have not love, I gain nothing. (1 Corinthians 13:1-3).
>
> Love must be sincere. Hate what is evil; cling to what is good. Be devoted to one another in agape love. Honor one another above yourselves. Never be lacking in zeal, but keep your spiritual fervor, serving the Lord. Be joyful in hope. Patient in affliction, faithful in prayer. Share with God's people who are in need. Practice hospitality. (Romans 12:9).
>
> Above all, love each other deeply, because love covers a multitude of sins. (1Peter 4:8).

Some Pentecostal churches demand speaking in tongues as evidence of true conversion. This is incorrect and should never have been instigated. It is clear from the above passages that God gives gifts according to his divine will and does not give the same to everyone. How could the Pentecostal teaching justify demanding of God that He gives a specific gift to everyone?

THE FIVEFOLD MINISTRY

Numbers are always significant in the Bible. The number five is a prime number and represents God's grace, goodness and favour toward humans, and His anointing. There were five wounds of Christ, five stones in David's pouch, and five loaves representing the bread of life. Now we have five ministries.

There are those who are called to the wider *ekklesia* and give leadership that transcends the ministry of small groups, yet at the same time equips, encourages, and supports those smaller groups. Such individuals will tend to operate beyond one single group of believers, ministering instead to the whole *ekklesia* in any given city and even beyond. In his letter to the Ephesians, Paul tells us that Christ has appointed five specific types of leadership (fivefold ministry) for this very purpose:

> "Christ himself gave the apostles, the prophets, the evangelists, the pastors and teachers, to equip his people for works of service, so that the body of Christ may be built up until we all reach unity in the faith and in the knowledge of the Son of God and become mature, attaining to the whole measure of the fullness of Christ." (Ephesians 4:11-13).

Only a few are called to the fivefold ministry. It is a higher calling, but still does not elevate the recipient to a status above the other believers. Like the elder and deacon discussed elsewhere, the individual must function as a servant leader. Those who accept this calling will be held to a higher account, so it is not to be taken lightly. Ezekiel describes how the shepherds (leaders) of Israel had led the people astray.

> "Woe to the shepherds of Israel who only take care of themselves. I am against the shepherds and will hold them accountable for my flock". (Ezekiel 34:2-10). I would not want to be in their shoes.

The five ministries are: Apostle, Prophet, Evangelist, Pastor, and Teacher.

Apostle

The word *apostle* comes from a Greek word *apostellos* that means, "set apart to send out on a mission by liberating from previous obligations" and "a sent one, a specially commissioned messenger of Jesus Christ." Its prefix "apo-" means "away from," to describe a separation where a sharp severing has taken place.

The original apostles were the twelve disciples Jesus called to follow him and whom he later commissioned to go into all the world with the gospel. An apostle as defined strictly by the New Testament no longer exists today, since these three conditions had to be met: the person had to have been an eyewitness to Jesus after his resurrection (1 Corinthians 9:1); he had to have been chosen by the Holy Spirit (Acts 9:15); and he had to have ministered with signs, miracles, and wonders (Acts 2:43; 2 Corinthians 12:12).

The apostle that Paul refers to as a component of the fivefold ministry is a person with apostolic gifting who not only serves the smaller groups of believers but also would typically function as a church planter—one sent out by the body of Christ to spread the gospel and establish new communities of believers. Anyone calling themselves "Apostle Fred" or "Apostle Jane" is, in my opinion, out of order and is the antithesis of a servant leader. You know apostles by their fruits, not by their title. This is applicable to all five of the ministries. An apostle does not build on the foundation of others; rather, they receive their own blueprint from the Lord. Being an apostle is not something you choose to be. It is a calling from God. Scripture does not refer to gender when distributing the gifts of the spirit. The Lord is only looking for willing vessels, ready to carry out His plan upon the earth, woman or man.

Prophet

Just as there were prophets during the Old Testament era, there were also prophets during the time of the New Testament. The task of the Old Testament prophet was not a happy one—it often carried with it a heavy price. (I don't suppose any of the Old Testament prophets enjoyed their calling.) God required them to deliver a message to the people that the audience did not want to hear! He sometimes asked them to do extraordinary things such as to go naked and without shoes for three years, demonstrating how the king of Assyria would end his days (Isaiah 20:3). The task of the New Testament prophets was similar to that of their Old Testament counterparts in that they were to speak forth the Word of God to the people. Today, those with prophetic gifting will speak forth encouragement to the people, less so to predict future events. Modern prophets continue to testify about Jesus. They also warn and advise us about important topics. If an individual claiming to be a prophet predicts what does not happen, he/she should be ignored.

Evangelist

An evangelist is someone who proclaims good news. A missionary is generally considered an evangelist. A person with the gift of evangelism may travel from place to place to preach the gospel. The title of an evangelist was applied to Philip in Acts 21:8.

Pastor

The word "pastor" derives from the Latin noun *pastor,* which means "shepherd" and from the verb *pascere*—"to lead to pasture, set to grazing, cause to eat." We get the word "pastoral" from this root as well. It is a wonderful image of a good shepherd leading his flock to water and pasture. One could expect an elder to be gifted as a pastor. Jesus was the original "Good Shepherd."

Teacher

While preaching and teaching are similar, there is the element of passion in declaring the gospel from the preacher. I am not sure if there is a role for preaching in the small group of believers; instead, this requires the making of disciples through quiet teaching. In such teaching there is the possibility of a two-way interaction with students asking questions for clarification. If there is no church building in the new *ekklesia*, the preacher may be seen on the street proclaiming the good news. I like the idea of specially gifted teachers travelling to different classrooms to give seminars on their chosen subject. We cannot all spend our lives buried in study books, learning Hebrew and Greek. It falls to the person gifted as a teacher to be the guide through theology at an appropriate level for his/her audience. I suppose there is also a subset of teachers not really mentioned in the Bible—the academic theologian. Into this category of teachers, we must somehow fit seminaries and training institutes for believers.

I have focused in other chapters on elements in religious Christianity that I consider inappropriate. In contrast, this chapter describes two essential elements (gifts and ministries) that the *ekklesia* needs if it is to bring the fullness of Christ into the world. Let us praise God for His grace toward us as He has granted us these wonderful gifts for the advancement of His Kingdom.

REFLECTIONS

Do you know what your gifting is? Have you been called to the fivefold ministry?

Do you think there are genuine apostles today, or just individuals who have an apostolic gift?

Do you know anyone in your ekklesia *who elevates himself/herself on account of his/her gifting? How do you feel toward them?*

In your ekklesia, *can you identify at least one person who is called to each of the fivefold gifts?*

Is speaking in tongues a genuine gift, or do people claim to have the gift but just make it up?

Do you know of someone who has prophesied something that has not come to pass?

10

THE GREAT COMMISSION

Jesus spoke to the eleven disciples after his Resurrection, telling them, "All authority in heaven and on earth has been given to me. Therefore, go and make disciples of all nations, baptizing them in the name of the Father and of the Son and of the Holy Spirit, and teaching them to obey everything I have commanded you. And surely, I am with you always, to the very end of the age." (Matthew 28:18-20). This passage is generally called the Great Commission.

Did Jesus want the gospel to be carried to all corners of the globe? I think so. Was he suggesting that it was only the eleven who should do this? I don't think so. It was an imperative for all believers for all times.

There have been generations of missionaries who have responded to the Great Commission and have left their own European or North American shores to spend their lives taking the gospel to other nations. The idea of a missionary really developed in the mid-nineteenth century. These brave souls left their hometowns, knowing it was unlikely they would ever return. Many died overseas, and some were even martyred. One can only have deep respect for these selfless acts.

Sadly, there was a side to such missionaries that is not often discussed. They were usually ordained in a particular church (be it Catholic or Protestant) and preached their denominational version of the gospel to the target audiences. As a result, swathes of developing nations have adopted denominationalism and have been taught an incomplete gospel. In addition, these missionaries have, often unwittingly, been the carriers of colonialism. This has been particularly evident in China and Africa where Western culture has invaded and often replace the local culture. Amazingly, countries that were originally the target for the nineteenth century missionaries (such as China and the Philippines) are now happily a major source of modern missionaries.

Newer, healthier models of missionary evangelism have emerged in recent years. Practically every developing nation has a diaspora, a small community in each of the West's large cities. Many will return to their country of birth from time to time, making them ideal "missionaries." If they can be encouraged to take the gospel with them on their trips home, they can have a profound effect on their family and friends. An Ethiopian I know in Melbourne has a small *ekklesia* round him. They send him back to Ethiopia several times a year where he meets with community leaders. He is not taking another culture to them, and he speaks in his mother tongue to them. He carries a lot of respect and has a huge impact on Christian leaders in that country.

But wait. How does this fit with the distribution of the ministry of evangelism that we talked about in Chapter 9, one member of the fivefold ministry? We now know we cannot leave it to the paid clergy whom we dismantled in Chapter 6! It must be up to us, the royal priests! I suggest there are at least three ways to answer the Great Commission.

First, there are Evangelists with a capital "E." They are few and far between; Billy Graham attracted thousands to each of his crusades, bringing the gospel to them. Another was Reinhart Bonke, a man to whom, in Reinhart's own words "God gave me Africa to evangelize." When he held a crusade in Africa, up to a million people at a time turned out to hear him. Such men and women are exceptional and can certainly be considered to operate in the ministry of evangelism.

Second, there are leaders in the city-wide *ekklesia* who operate in the gift of evangelism through presenting the gospel on the street or at meetings beyond a single house church. We should expect to see at least one example of this in every city eldership.

Third, there is the evangelism that we must all embrace. It is probably the hardest dimension of Christian life to fulfill. It is the way we live. We can even tell people about the gospel! But many in the church have not had a life-impacting encounter with God that propels them to want to share the gospel. Instead, people are simply being introduced into church life. Too often, the church does not lead people to a place where they truly encounter God.

The second commandment is to love one another. If we show love to other Christians and non-Christians, we are living the life of an evangelist. We are perpetually on show to the world. They must see a difference between us and the world. Even small children know "humbug," an insincere person when they see one. Our agape love must be from our hearts, not a shallow performance we switch on at just the right moment. We may never actually mention the gospel. But a neighbour may ask, "What is different about you?" or a similar question that opens the door to disclosing the gospel to them.

I worked for some years as a volunteer chaplain in a busy general hospital. The fact that people were in the hospital probably meant they had had or were in the middle of a life-threatening event. They were being confronted by their own mortality, something most of us manage to suppress in our everyday lives. This is a "niche market" when individuals are more open than usual to discuss their faith and what they imagine their afterlife will look like.

In the deconstructed religious church that I have described in this short book, I encourage each one of us to accept the responsibility of the third type of evangelism, to allow our lives to be an advertisement for the Kingdom of God. If the Holy Spirit opens an opportunity to speak about the gospel, wonderful. But we should not be concerned if our lives and our actions are the dominant tools of evangelism instead of our words.

I have found parenting to be a sobering experience for character-building. My two sons have taken little notice of what I have said to them or *told* them what to do. They have taken much more notice of what I have *done* in my life. But I believe the only significant impact I have had on their development has been *who I am*. Getting my character right has been a lifelong work. However hard I try to conceal my imperfections, my character is visible for all to see.

Evangelism is looking outwards, not inwards to the existing members of our *ekklesia* who have already heard the gospel. I have offered the example of the life you lead as the best tool you have to evangelize. But there are simple acts that can complement that life on display. They might include stopping on the stairs of your apartment block to get to know your neighbours. You could invite a few acquaintances round for coffee or a meal. But don't make it difficult. Don't practice what you might say to introduce the gospel. *It is not your responsibility*. Let the Holy Spirit open doors. He will give you all the words you need at the right time if you avoid trying to do it in your own strength. After all, in the passage I have quoted above, Jesus said "I am with you always, to the very end of the age." Let him do the work.

REFLECTIONS

If you were to be accused of being a Christian, would there be enough evidence to convict you? Is Christ evident for others to see in your life?

As a royal priest, how can you take the gospel to others?

Evangelism is too difficult for ordinary Christians, isn't it?

How do character inconsistencies, domestic violence, drug-taking, drunkenness and other inconsiderate behaviours affect evangelism?

Can you have a "day off" from being a Christian?

Can you identify a person in your city whom you consider is an evangelist?

How does your church attract people so that they keep coming every Sunday?

11

THE INCOMPLETE REFORMATION

Previous chapters have referred to the church having drifted off course in various ways and at various times. Some of the course changes have been minimal while others have been catastrophically huge! The history of the church since Pentecost is a gigantic subject, and I will try and summarize it with only essential points. By doing so, I readily concede that there are historians, better writers by far than I, who have produced enormous tomes on the subject, and my own brief description is in danger of trivializing the subject. That is not my intention, but I simply wish to focus on the more obvious trends that have emerged over the centuries.

FIRST CENTURY

The start of the Church Era, as it is called, began with the ascension of Jesus and the giving of the Holy Spirit to those assembled in the upper room at Pentecost (Acts 2). The number of believers grew rapidly (Acts 2), and they began meeting in private homes.

SECOND CENTURY

By the turn of the first century, we know that Christians were meeting in homes, but there was also cohesion within cities. Jesus speaks to seven churches in Asia Minor in Revelation 2, prefacing his remarks by "the church in Ephesus" and the "church in Philadelphia." It is unlikely there was just one home being used for all Christians in each city; rather, there must have been some measure of cohesion in the Christian community that allowed communication between groups. Persecution resulted in great unity. Early bishops/elders emerged such as Ignatius and Polycarp.

THIRD CENTURY

The Roman Empire persecuted Christians, creating martyrs by killing and torturing them including burning them as a public spectacle. Persecution of Christians began as early as 54AD under Nero and continued right up until the Emperor Constantine issued the Edict of Milan in 313AD, allowing tolerance of all religions including Christianity. Probably the worst period was under Emperor Diocletian 283-305AD, resulting in the "Great Persecution." Christians were driven underground to practice their faith, yet their numbers continued to increase.

FOURTH CENTURY

Christianity flourished despite persecution. But in 315AD, it became the official religion of the Roman Empire. Roman state authority blended with that of the church. By this time, a hierarchical system of clergy and laity had emerged with bishops in each of the great centres. Augustine of Hippo in North Africa (354-430) was an example of this. The greatest perversion of the meaning of the word *ekklesia*, in my opinion, was brought about by the Emperor Constantine. Christians were seen as a threat to the rule of the emperors who dealt with them in the most severe manner. Nonetheless, the faith flourished in the face of this persecution. Now it is told that Constantine had a conversion experience, and he supposedly gave his life to Christ. Who am I to argue? At the proper time, he will be judged on that issue. But forgive me if I am a little skeptical.

In 315AD he declared Christianity to be the religion of the Roman Empire. The very fact that he had gained the status of Emperor meant Constantine was an ace politician and an accomplished strategist. The rule of the Empire changed hands so quickly and many transitions of power were stained with blood. Emperors to a man were ruthless. The logical thing for Constantine to have done was just to leave Christians alone and not persecute them. But he went much further and insisted everyone had to become Christian. I think he saw huge personal advantage in not only stopping the unrest caused by Christians, but also, by making them mainstream, he gained control of the blossoming faith. If you can't beat them, join them. He converted pagan temples into Christian places of worship (churches) and made everyone who was pagan convert to Christianity. The faith was immediately diluted with forced converts whose genuine faith was uncertain. With these former pagans came all their pagan practices which I describe in another chapter. This was the origin of the Roman Catholic Church. Its headquarters were originally in Constantinople, but with the split in the Empire, that was moved to Rome, leaving the Eastern Church under the control of others. Constantine now controlled the secular and the religious sectors of the Empire.

THE GREAT SCHISM

Many major Churches of the East claim to have been founded by the apostles: Alexandria by Mark, Constantinople by Andrew, Cyprus by Barnabas, Ethiopia by Matthew, India by Thomas, Edessa in eastern Syria by Thaddeus, Armenia by Bartholomew, and Georgia by Simon the Zealot. Over a 37-year period from 482 to 519, these Eastern Orthodox Churches gradually split from the Western (Roman) Church. Disputes about theological and other questions of authority ultimately led to schisms between the Churches in Rome and Constantinople. The separation between East and West was evident from 866–879, each side refusing to be ruled by the other.

DARK AGES

With the weakening of the Western Roman Empire militarily to the fracturing of the church in the Great Schism, Europe was plunged into darkness. It became known as the Dark Ages and lasted from around 500AD to 1500AD. It was the church's equivalent of the Babylonian captivity. It was an age of corruption and substitution, with all key elements of Christianity being eroded. With knowledge and encouragement from the Pope, armies from Europe undertook the great crusades against the Middle East's conversion to Islam. At home, the Catholic Inquisition sought out anyone questioning Catholic doctrine and tortured or executed them. The Catholic translation of the Bible into Latin was known as the Vulgate and was the only translation permissible. It remained in the control of the clergy, oftentimes being chained closed to ensure the laity did not get a chance to read it. Mass was conducted in Latin, thereby further limiting the congregation's understanding. This all increased the dependence of the people on the clergy to interpret the Bible for them.

THE REFORMATION

On 31 October 1517, a monk in Wittenberg called Martin Luther nailed 95 theses to the church door discrediting "indulgences," payments for the forgiveness of sins. Luther's indignation at Rome for this monstrous system was the first trickle of reformation. It soon became a flood. Despite Luther's being a Catholic priest who only wanted to change a few specifics in the church, others were triggered to make far more radical moves away from the Roman Catholic Church. These protesters (Protestants) identified many different points of controversy and began forming their own churches. I deal with the emergence of denominations in another chapter.

THE INCOMPLETE REFORMATION

As radical as the Reformation was after Luther's brave declarations, the Catholic Church battled on, largely unscathed. It roundly condemned

Luther for his views and countered with its own declaration of the sanctity of Catholic doctrine at the Council of Trent (between 1545 and 1563). The resulting Protestant churches, while claiming aversion to Rome, nevertheless still looked a lot like the Catholic Church. For instance, instead of the Pope, there was (in the case of the Anglican Church), a king and archbishop who controlled the church, and instead of the priest there was either a vicar, a pastor, or one with a similar title who oversaw the congregation. Protestant meetings were generally held in designated buildings/churches whose structure was barely distinguishable from the Catholic church. Even the services were much the same, although they would be held in a local language and not Latin.

Luther was not the first person to realize there was something wrong with the Catholic Church. Others had gone before and paid a high price. But Luther pulled away at a huge brick in the papal wall, and without intending it, he joined the process already started by many others to distance themselves from Catholicism. Despite this attempt to deconstruct the church, the Roman wall is largely unscathed today.

Sadly, the post-reformation Protestant church, for the most part, perpetuated the person of the priest, ignoring the teaching of the "priesthood of all believers." It perpetuated the hierarchical system for church leadership. And the division between the clergy and laity remained largely unchanged. Church meetings were as rigid as before with the people passively stuck in pews while the clergy ran the service. The Reformation had done well but was incomplete. It remains incomplete to this day. Instead, we have the legacy of a plethora of denominations.

THE GOOD NEWS!

I am not the first person to come to the realization that the church (can we call them the *ekklesia*?) has deviated from the original New Testament design and endeavoured to replace the temple worship with our own version. Despite great efforts to break away from the Roman model, Protestants have clung onto much of the Catholic tradition. I am only repeating in my own words what many have written before me. Happily, over the years even before Luther, there were many streams of Christians who have rejected both Catholic and Protestant ways. They have maintained a simpler method of expressing their faith. Perhaps we can take a lesson from them.

REFLECTIONS

Was the church united before the Reformation?

Was it wrong for the reformers to cause disunity in Christendom by pulling away from Catholicism?

Do you agree that the Reformation is incomplete? What would it take to complete it? Is it just too difficult?

12

DENOMINATIONS, SECTS AND CULTS

Until the Reformation, the church was basically divided only into East and West. But from the Reformation onward, large numbers of denominations emerged. Sadly, these splits caused walls of division, not bridges of unity. Psalm 133 tells us: "How good and pleasant it is when God's people live together in unity." But tragically, there seems to be little unity in Christendom today.

DENOMINATIONS

A denomination in Christianity is an organization (an association or fellowship) that unites local congregations into a single legal and administrative body. Members of each denomination share the same beliefs or creed, participate in similar worship practices, and cooperate together to develop and preserve shared enterprises. The word denomination comes from the Latin *denominare* meaning "to name." Most Christian denominations self-describe themselves as *Churches*, whereas some newer ones tend to use the terms churches, assemblies, or fellowships interchangeably.

SECTS

Sects are not the same as denominations. Sects can be considered as religious groups that have formed to protest elements of their parent denomination. Their motivation tends to be accusations of apostasy or heresy against the parent denomination. They often complain of liberal trends in the parent denomination and advocate a return to true religion. Sects tend to claim to be an authentic, purged, refurbished version of the faith from which they split. Sects generally claim to possess unique and privileged access to the truth or salvation, and their committed adherents typically regard all those outside the sect as "in error." Sects are rarely recognised by parent faiths.

Initially Christianity was considered a sect of Judaism (Acts 24:5). In the second century there was no organised Christian religion, hence no denominations. As Christianity developed, so did denominations. One of the earliest signs of a split within the main church was the controversy caused by Nestorians who overemphasized the human nature of Jesus at the expense of the divine. At the Council of Ephesus in 431AD, approximately two hundred bishops were present to discuss this division. The proceedings were conducted in a heated atmosphere of confrontation and recriminations.

Until the Reformation, the Christian church was basically divided into Coptic, Eastern Orthodox and Western Roman Catholics. We discuss elsewhere the reasons for the split between the Eastern and Western churches called the Great Schism. As a consequence of the Reformation, Protestant churches emerged. These included Anabaptists, Mennonite and Amish, Anglican, Methodist and Quaker, Congregationalist and Baptist, Lutheran and Evangelical, Reformed and Presbyterian, Pentecostal and Non-denominational. Each of these has generated a raft of other denominations.

In response to the Reformation, the Roman Catholic Church convened the Council of Trent. It was held between 1545AD and 1563AD in Trent (or Trento) in northern Italy. It was the Catholic Church's attempt to counter the claims made by the Protestant reformers. It has been described as the embodiment of the Counter-Reformation. The Council issued condemnations of what it defined as heresies committed by proponents of Protestantism, and it also issued key statements and clarifications of the Church's doctrine and teachings. In other words, the Roman Catholic Church dug its heels in!

"Reformed" Christianity developed in Switzerland based on the teachings of Ulrich Zwingli and John Calvin. When it spread to Scotland under John Knox, the Reformed faith became Presbyterianism. Switzerland was also the birthplace of the Anabaptists, spiritual ancestors of today's Amish, Mennonites, Quakers, and Baptists.

Those who remained within the fold of Roman Catholicism during the Reformation argued that the central regulation of doctrine was necessary to prevent confusion and division within the church and corruption of beliefs. Protestants, on the other hand, insisted that it was precisely this policy of control that had already led to corruption of the true faith. The reformers demanded that believers be allowed to read the Scriptures for themselves in their own language (it was previously available only in Latin and with restricted access to the book) and to act in accordance with their conscience. This issue of religious authority continues to be a fundamental difference in perspective between Catholic and Orthodox Christians on one hand and Protestant Christians on the other.

The Anglican Church is a Protestant church originating in the UK and was born out of rebellion to the Catholic Church and the Papacy. It was established in 1534 when England's King Henry VIII broke from the authority of the Pope. Anglicanism is often regarded as a "Middle Way" between Catholicism and Protestantism, while others categorize it as Protestant. Anglicanism became Episcopalianism in the United States. Methodism, based on the teachings of John Wesley, also has its roots in Anglicanism.

With its emphasis on individual interpretation of scripture and a measure of religious freedom, the Reformation marked not only a break between Protestantism and Catholicism, but also the beginning of Christian denominationalism. Today, Christianity encompasses an astounding variety of denominations, sects, and churches. Relationships between these groups range from mutual respect and cooperation to denial that the other group is really "Christian." Many Christian groups would also refuse the label of "Christian denomination," considering themselves the *only* true form of Christianity, not one among many.

How the denominations are divided up[11]

The approximate distribution of Protestants making the 36.7% is as follows:

Pentecostals	105,000,000
Baptists	105,000,000
Non-denominational	80,000,000
Methodists	75,000,000
Lutheran	75,000,000
Presbyterian/Reform	75,000,000
Anglican/Episcopalian	70,000,000
Adventists	15,500,000
Anabaptists	5,000,000
Church of Christ	5,000,000

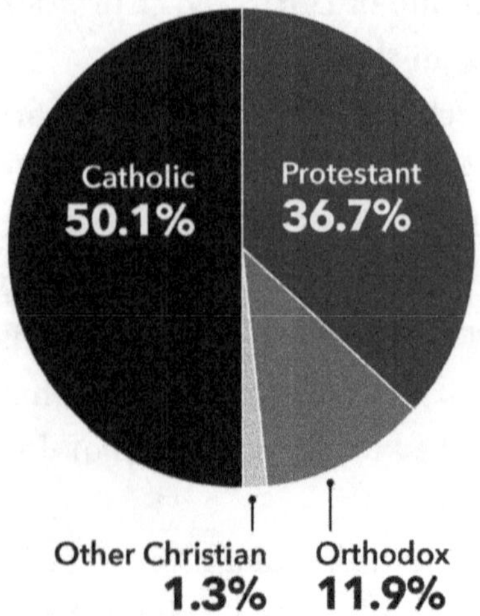

[11] Source: Pew-Templeton Global Religious Futures Project (December 2011). Global Christianity: A Report on the Size and Distribution of the World's Christian Population. https://assets.pewresearch.org/wp-content/uploads/sites/11/2011/12/Christianity-fullreport-web.pdf

The exact number of Christian denominations is uncertain as more are being created all the time. Wikipedia[12] claims there are more than 45,000 denominations globally. Why are there so many? Divisions between one group and another are defined in general by authority and doctrinal issues such as:

- The nature of Jesus
- The authority of apostolic succession
- Biblical hermeneutics
- Theology
- Ecclesiology
- Eschatology
- Papal primacy

Denominations tend to stress one teaching or aspect of doctrine (e.g., baptism, deliverance) rather than a full, balanced gospel.

Although one can rationalize the creation of denominations with high-minded reasons such as those I have outlined above, I believe there is a much darker malaise that underpins these disputes. I suspect some of the underlying drivers to the formation of denominations have been:

- Pride—I know better than you what is right.
- Political expediency
- Authority, desire for control, power, money
- Rebellion
    - I don't want to do it your way. I want to do it my way. My interpretation of scriptures indicates to me that I have a better understanding of the Bible than you,

[12] https://www.google.com/search?q=number+of+Chrsitian+denomantions%2C+-cults+and+sects&oq=number+of+Chrsitian+denomantions%2C+cults+and+sects&aqs=-chrome..69i57.16237j0j15&sourceid=chrome&ie=

  and I will set up an organization where I am the boss and I lead people in my way.
  - You are doing it wrong; consequently, you are all heretics.
- The need for belonging to a tribe and needing a leader (even if that leader is a false teacher).
- Gullibility—being led by a false teacher who rides on the back of poor biblical understanding by the people
- The opposite of servant leadership
- Satan's ability to pervert anything God is doing

There are, of course, consequences of forming denominations. The most profound is the disunity it generates in the Body of Christ. This is one of the principal reasons I hear of people rejecting everything the "Church" stands for. Over the history of the church, terrible things have been perpetrated in the name of denominations such as the Inquisition, persecution of other expressions of Christianity e.g., the Cathars, killings and burning at the stake of supposed heretics, and displacement of populations in the face of persecution or prohibition to practice their faith e.g., the Huguenots.

CULTS

Cults generally have roots in Gnosticism and the ancient Jewish Kabbalah. It is a collection of religious ideas and systems which came together in the late 1st century AD among Jewish and early Christian sects. These various groups emphasized personal (often secret) spiritual knowledge above the orthodox teachings, traditions, and authority of the Church. A cult is a system of religious veneration and devotion directed toward a particular figure or object. It is usually a relatively small group of people having religious principles or practices regarded by others as strange, deviant, or sinister, and the cult often includes an excessive admiration for a particular person or thing. The gospel of Jesus is generally added to, subtracted from, or perverted in some way. Proponents of the cult tend to deny the trinity, the deity of Christ, the bodily resurrection of Christ or salvation by grace, or all of the above. Cults are incompatible with Christianity but often claim to be Christian.

Some examples of groups calling themselves Christian but whose doctrine reveals such divergence from the gospel that they should not be included in the list of true Christians are the Mormons, Christian Scientists, Jehovah's Witnesses, Seventh Day Adventists, and Unitarians. I consider that Roman Catholicism diverges so far from the gospel on fundamental points that it is questionable whether it is Christian or not. I will leave the reader to examine the facts and make his/her own mind up.

IN SUMMARY

There is little positive about denominations. "*In an increasingly hostile secular culture, we in the 21st century Western church must examine the cause of the ekklesia's malaise, and radically re-cast the Christian vision for the 21st century. What is required is nothing short of the recovery of the biblical vision for a kingdom-shaped ekklesia; designed and destined by God to transform entire cultures and disciple nations. Even so, until God's people repent of the scandal of their sectarian divisions—albeit in the name of orthodoxy or pragmatism—the world will not listen. Only when we understand the revelation of the unity of God (Deuteronomy 6:4-5; Mark 12:29; Ephesians 4:4-6), and become one body, one Spirit and one faith, will God entrust to us the spiritual authority needed for the full harvest of the nations.*" David Orton 2020.

Do any of the above denominations, sects or cults constitute a false religion? The reader must decide for him/herself on that. In 1 John 4:2 it says, "This is how you can recognise the Spirit of God. Every spirit that acknowledges that Jesus Christ has come in the flesh is from God, but every spirit that does not acknowledge Jesus is not from God." That is a good starting point, but is it enough to determine the authenticity of a denomination? If you believe in Jesus and in addition, pray to Mary and the saints, is that OK?

I would not want to be a part of a false religion, nor would I want to lead others astray. Revelation 17 describes false belief systems of the world in no uncertain manner. The woman on the beast is "Babylon the great, the mother of prostitutes and the abomination of the earth." She represents all the false religions of the world.

The famous Chinese evangelist Watchman Nee has some strong words to say about the denominations that he saw in the European missionaries' versions of Christianity. He "*found the Christians of the missionary societies' churches half-hearted and compromising and charged that the denominations were weighted down with what was to him man-made traditions regarding baptism, worship and ordination, teaching what was quite foreign to what he read in the New Testament.*"[13]

David Orton again: "*The call is for radical repentance and reformation—a rending of our hearts and a mending of our ways; the dismantling of false belief systems and idolatrous power structures that resist the knowledge of God. It cries out for false theologies and the scandal of denominationalism to be addressed.*"14

REFLECTIONS

Has the motivation for forming denominations been wrong? Often individuals such as Luther have seen errors in the parent church that are unacceptable to them. They want to fix it. They create their own version of the parent church, usually with only minor changes toward incremental improvement. That can't be bad, can it? One can imagine God placing on that individual's heart the desire for something better. My concern about that scenario is that I consider the church hierarchical system to be flawed, so replacing it with another hierarchical system is probably not advancing His Kingdom much.

[13] Norman H. Cliff, "Watchman Nee-- Church Planter and Preacher of Holiness," *Evangelical Review of Theology*, Vol.8 No. 2 (Oct. 1984): p. 290.

[14] David Orton. Lifemessenger.org

Are all denominations bad, and is everyone in a denomination evil? Of course not. God has always used men and women in their imperfection (take King David, for example). If you are in, for instance, a Methodist church, you can still be filled with the Holy Spirit, hear what God is saying to you, and respond accordingly. You can still be a sincere Christian in your denominational church.

Is there an intermediate step we can take? Perhaps ensuring that from the denomination in which we worship, we extend love across boundaries and not judge too harshly those of a different persuasion?

Will denominational churches ever cease to exist? I don't think so. My personal estimate is that there will always be the main denominational churches around. But they will shrink to a fraction of their current size and influence, maintained by people who do not want to hear the new thing God is doing.

Does God call everyone who is in a denominational church to come out? Like the Jews in Babylon, it may be too hard for most to leave what they are used to. I don't believe He will judge anyone for that. But He does call a remnant to come out of the place they have been comfortable in. He has always called a remnant out (see Chapter 17).

Will some other type of assembly replace denominational churches? Only God knows. But we get a glimpse of what may emerge from the underground Christian movements of China, of house churches, home churches, street churches and beach churches. These are often spontaneous expressions of the faith of a small group of like-minded people. They will refuse to be named or pigeon-holed. No ordained priest will be in charge, but they will rely on the Holy Spirit for leadership.

Will it be wonderful to be a "called-out-one" and leave your denomination? I'm not so sure. Be warned what God has said He will do for his remnant; "This third I will bring into the fire. I will refine them like gold. They will call on my name and I will answer them; I will say, 'They are my people', and they will say, 'The Lord is our God.'" (Zechariah 13:9). Do you want to have the dross burned out of you like the refining of gold? Ouch.

When will all this happen? The shift away from denominations has already begun. But when will the seismic shift (the big shaking) occur? Next week, next year, next decade? Who knows? Only God.

13

ECUMENISM, MULTIFAITH, AND INTERFAITH MOVEMENTS

As the deluge of denominations that were created after the Reformation, individuals emerged who recognized the need to try and re-unite Christendom. In response, there arose the Ecumenical Movement. Ecumenism is the principle of promoting unity among the world's Christian communities. It refers to efforts among Christian bodies to develop better understandings and closer relationships. It also refers to efforts toward visible unity in the Christian Church. This chapter is the necessary sequel to the one on denominationalism as it offers the potential for uniting what is disunited, namely the Body of Christ.

If all the main churches accept the basics of the faith, surely is there not enough there to bring them together and overcome their differences? You might think so. The enthusiasm with which this concept was embraced in 1937 and then in the post-war period resulted in the formation of the World Council of Churches (WCC). The headquarters were built in Geneva, Switzerland, literally down the road from the United Nations Headquarters, symbolically paralleling the secular task of the UN to work with all nations toward world peace and the avoidance of another global conflict. There were 349 churches working together to this end. As well as doctrinal and theological issues, the WCC acted against Apartheid in the 1970s and

1980s. A sister organization was formed in Asia called the Christian Conference of Asia (CCA), which provided active resistance against Ferdinand Marcos in the Philippines.

Sadly, the conditions required for this unity have varied from church to church, but most distressing is the condition set by the Roman Catholic Church and Eastern Orthodox Church, both teaching visible unity may only be achieved by converting to their denominational beliefs and structure, citing claims of being the one true church.

Even if all post-Reformation denominations agreed to unite, still the bulk of Christianity (the Roman Catholic and Orthodox congregations) would not join.

Does it matter if we are not all in unity? Well, yes, it does. Biblically all Christians are called to unite: "My prayer is not for them alone. I pray also for those who will believe in me through their message that all of them may be one..." (John 17:20). Jesus goes on to say WHY Christians must be united: "...so that the world may believe that you have sent me. I have given them the glory that you gave me, that they may be one as we are one. May they be brought to complete unity to let the world know that you sent me and have loved them even as you have loved me." (John 17:22-23)

If we are in any doubt about the imperative Jesus gives us to be united, He does it again in John 13:34: "A new command I give you: love one another. As I have loved you, so you must love one another. By this, all men will know that you are my disciples if you love one another."

The WCC has been doing its best for 70 years with little to show for its efforts in terms of real progress. Maybe that is not the way to achieve God's goal. I mean no disrespect to the great men and women who have laboured in the organization.

MULTIFAITH

While I can respect the efforts and goals of those involved in ecumenism, I feel differently about multifaith. This movement promotes the idea that we should express an affinity towards other religions, philosophies, or world views, and perhaps to believe that no one faith is superior to any of the others. This is incompatible with Christianity. Faith in Jesus cannot be equated with the Muslim or Buddhist faiths. Again, no disrespect is intended towards the faithful of those religions.

INTERFAITH

Interfaith is the process of communicating with those from other religions, presumably obeying the command to love our neighbour. Such efforts have generated harmony between faith communities and racial groups and has had a very positive effect. There is a real danger, however, that Interfaith activities extend beyond social harmony and mutual understanding to become a multifaith exercise. It is a fine line between the two activities.

THE GLOOMY TRUTH

So how can we Christians achieve true unity? Clearly (and sadly), it is obvious that this will not be accomplished through the WCC or similar organizational approaches. Simply amalgamating several denominations into one slightly larger denomination does not solve the problem, however well-meaning it may be. I believe that for as long as denominations persist in Christianity, it will be impossible to achieve unity. There cannot be denominations and unity at the same time because they are incompatible. Of course, there will always be cultural variations in how people express themselves before the Lord. And I am sure He loves that.

REFLECTIONS

Is there value in continuing to pursue ecumenism, even though it has not produced tangible results to date?

Should we be satisfied simply to get along better with other denominations?

Can denominations be deconstructed/abolished? No, not by human endeavour. I believe that unless there is divine intervention, it will not happen. Christianity will need to be shaken to its core before progress is to be made. What will that shaking look like? I don't know. When will it happen? I don't know.

14

FALSE TEACHERS

I have identified the ministry of teaching as one of the fivefold ministry. But not all teachers are equal. The Body of Christ today is led by good teachers and bad. There will always be those who lead the flock astray—the Bible warns repeatedly about false teachers. Every Christian needs to be alert to the possibility they may be unwittingly following such false teachers. Some leaders are downright corrupt and lead unsuspecting individuals into cults. Others misrepresent the gospel in apparently minor errors that have far-reaching consequences. Especially, readers of this book need to consider whether you are being led astray by what I write. Test everything against Scripture.

We are warned in Revelation 22 that we are not to accept any alteration to the text of the Bible nor any omission or (especially) any addition. In other words, teachers who claim to have special revelation SUBSEQUENT TO the closing of the canon. i.e., after the last chapter of Revelation, are to be considered false teachers and disregarded.

Many modern evangelists and preachers espouse what is known as the "prosperity gospel." This teaches that if you "sow" into my ministry, you will receive financial reward many-fold greater than your original gift. For "sow," read "give money to me." Famous evangelists and especially tele-evangelists are well known for this. They include such high-profile figures as Benny Hinn, Kenneth Copeland, Creflo Dollar (who would have thought with a name like that?), Joyce Meyer, and Jesse Duplantis. Many of them have become exceedingly rich, the richest being reputedly worth $760 million. Another, worth only $50 million, brags about owning his own plane so he can get to speaking engagements more easily. These characters are obscenely rich and bring the Christian faith into disrepute.

It is not just the individual evangelists who are rich. The church organizations themselves have often amassed huge fortunes—and for what purpose? In the Middle Ages in England, certain monasteries controlled the wool industry and became rich. They built glorious buildings with the money, even if the monks themselves lived modest lives. Today, major churches are incredibly rich with assets in the billions of dollars. For example, Wikipedia notes that the Catholic Church in Rome is worth 16 billion dollars, and the Church of Jesus Christ of Latter-Day Saints (Mormons) may be worth up to 100 billion dollars in assets. The Church of England (Anglican) may be worth 7.8 billion dollars and the Church of Scientology a mere 2 billion dollars.

The gospel has been "tampered with" in various ways. And we Christians must be alert to this process. Many churches believe that they have a special revelation that becomes their focus. For example, some churches include "deliverance" in their title. This means they offer a deliverance ministry as their main draw card. As deliverance was part of Jesus' ministry, it goes without saying that all Christian communities should be capable of offering this. The deliverance churches major on the minor instead of focusing on the whole gospel. Similarly, there are churches in the USA who focus on snakes, quoting Luke 10:18 that says "I saw Satan fall like lightning from heaven. I have given you authority to trample on snakes and scorpions and to overcome all the power of the enemy; nothing will harm you." I think Jesus was speaking figuratively here and did not expect everyone to rush out and stamp on snakes with impunity. Beware the incomplete gospel or the gospel that is unbalanced.

Another way the gospel is distorted is by adding to it, contrary to specific instructions in Revelation 22:18, indicating a curse to anyone who does. Take for example, the Mormon Church which was founded on revelations given to Joseph Smith on the night of 21 September 1823. The revelation was given to him by a heavenly messenger who gave his name as Moroni and revealed the existence

of an ancient record containing the fullness of the Gospel of Christ. This revelation became the "Book of Mormon" subtitled "Another Testament of Jesus Christ." Jehovah's Witnesses have their own (false) version of the bible. We deal with cults in Chapter 11.

I am convinced that false teaching is not only prevalent today in Christian churches, but also that millions of Christians have been deceived by these teachers to the extent that I question whether they have actually accepted the true gospel. For this reason, I have devoted some space to emphasizing how important the issue is as revealed in the Bible. Here are four of the common false teachings—that every one should be rich and healthy (Prosperity gospel), that extra rules have been added (e.g. speaking in tongues is necessary to be saved), that there is an over-stress on grace and love, omitting the holiness of God (I can do anything and God will forgive me), and that finally, if you sow into my ministry, you will be healed.

Here are some truths about false teaching:

> *"Today's church cannot remain faithful if it tolerates false teachers and leaves their teachings uncorrected and unconfronted."* Albert Mohler.
>
> *"You can believe in whatsoever you like, but the truth remains the truth, no matter how sweet the lie may taste."* Michael Bassey Johnson.
>
> *"If a person claims, "Thus says the Lord," and tells you something but it contradicts the Bible, it is not the truth."* Dexsta Ray.

Why do teachers preach less or more of the gospel? In the second chapter of Peter's second epistle, he identifies three key motivations: pride/power, sex, and money—nothing new here!

- Pride, or defying authority (verse 10) — verse 1: they deny "the Master who bought them" (also verses 12–13 and 18).
- Sensuality, which typically means sexual sin — verse 2: "many will follow their sensuality" (verses 10, 12–14, and 19).
- Greed, for money and material gain — verse 3: "in their greed they will exploit you" (also verses 14–15). For many it is a get rich quick scheme. Others don't speak the truth because that will cause people to leave their church. Less people in pews may mean less money. "These people always cause trouble. Their minds are corrupt, and they have turned their backs on the truth. To them, a show of godliness is just a way to become wealthy." (1 Timothy 6:5).

The "genuine" prophets in the Old Testament talk about false prophets (1 Kings 22:1-12; Isaiah 9:15; 28:7; Jeremiah 5:31; 6:13; 23:1-40; Ezekiel 13:3-4). Ezekiel says: "My hand will be against the prophets who see false visions and utter lying divinations. They will not belong to the council of my people or be listed in the records of Israel, nor will they enter the land of Israel. Then you will know that I am the Sovereign LORD. This is what the Sovereign Lord says: Woe to the shepherds of Israel who only take care of themselves. I am against the shepherds and will hold them accountable for my flock. I will remove them from tending my flock." (Ezekiel 13:9)

"Those who guide this people mislead them, and those who are guided are led astray." (Isaiah 9:16).

And Jeremiah says: Woe to the shepherds who are destroying and scattering the sheep of my pasture. (Jerimiah 12:1). And: This is what the LORD Almighty says: "Do not listen to what the prophets are prophesying to you; they fill you with false hopes. They speak visions from their own minds, not from the mouth of the LORD. (Jeremiah 22:16).

Jesus also warned of false prophets (Matthew 7:15-23; 24:11-28). Jesus comes at the subject from several angles. "Beware of false prophets who come disguised as harmless sheep but are really vicious wolves. You can identify them by their fruit, that is, by the way they act. Can you pick grapes from thornbushes, or figs from thistles? A good tree produces good fruit, and a bad tree produces bad fruit. Likewise, every good tree bears good fruit, but a bad tree bears bad fruit. A good tree cannot bear bad fruit, and a bad tree cannot bear good fruit. Every tree that does not bear good fruit is cut down and thrown into the fire. Thus, by their fruit you will recognize them. (Matthew 7;17).

"Their fruit" are identified in Galatians 5:22: Love. Joy. Peace. Longsuffering. Kindness. Goodness. Faithfulness. Gentleness. Self-control. If these fruits are lacking in the life of the teacher or the prophet, we should discount anything they teach.

Jesus was very specific about whom he was talking. "How is it you don't understand that I was not talking to you about bread? But be on your guard against the yeast of the Pharisees and Sadducees." Then they understood that he was not telling them to guard against the yeast used in bread, but against the teaching of the Pharisees and Sadducees." (Matthew 16:11-12).

"Watch out for the teachers of the law. They like to walk round in flowing robes and be greeted in the marketplaces and have the most important seats in the synagogues and the places of honor at the banquets. They devour widows' houses and for a show make lengthy prayers. Such men will be punished most severely." (Mark 12:38).

The apostles also had much to say about false prophets and teachers (Acts 20:28-35; 2 Corinthians 11:3–12:13; Galatians 1:6-9; Philippians 3:1-2; Colossians 2:8-15; 1 Thessalonians 1:3-12; 1 Timothy 1:3-7; 6:3-5; 2 Timothy 2:14-26; 3:2-8, 13; 4:14-18; Titus 1:10-16; 3:9-11; 1 John 2:18-29; 3:2-12; 4:1-6; 2 John 7-11; 3 John 9-10; Jude).

Paul speaks to the Ephesians. "Keep watch over yourselves and all the flock of which the Holy Spirit has made you overseers. Be shepherds of the church of God, which he bought with his own blood. I know that after I leave, savage wolves will come in among you and will not spare the flock. Even from your own number men will arise and distort the truth to draw away disciples after them." (Acts 20:28-30).

"For the time will come when people will not put up with sound doctrine. Instead, to suit their own desires, they will gather around them a great number of teachers to say what their itching ears want to hear. They will turn their ears away from the truth and turn aside to myths." (I Timothy 4:3-4).

"Dear friends, do not believe every spirit, but test the spirits to see whether they are from God, because many false prophets have gone out into the world. This is how you can recognize the Spirit of God: Every spirit that acknowledges that Jesus Christ has come in the flesh is from God, but *every spirit that does not acknowledge Jesus is not from God*. This is the spirit of the antichrist, which you have heard is coming and even now is already in the world." (1 John 4:1).

How can we recognise false teaching and false teachers? Here are some pointers.

- By revelation
- By their fruits
- By their failure to acknowledge Jesus as Saviour and Son of God
- By prophecies that are not fulfilled
- By the character of the teacher (greed, acquisition of property etc.)
- By contradiction of biblical truths
- They take care of themselves and exalt themselves
- They draw people away from the truth and form e.g., sects
- They add to the scriptures

While Christian leaders have a responsibility to guard the flock from false teachers (Acts 20:28-39; 1 Timothy 1:3-11; 2 Timothy 2:23-26), this does not absolve us of our personal responsibility to be on guard against false teachers.

False teachers have caused havoc in the church since the time of Jesus and continue to do so today. I consider the danger from within is at least as great as the danger from without. There is only one way we will be able to spot false teachers: we must be knowledgeable concerning the truth of the Word of God. We dare not become lazy and expect others to do our studying and thinking for us. We must evaluate everything against scripture. Personal preferences and individual opinions do not come into such an evaluation.

REFLECTIONS

Have you personally been led astray by false teachers?

Does this book constitute false teaching? I must take responsibility for writing it, and you, dear reader, must take responsibility for evaluating it against scripture.

15

SHAKING THE CHURCH

If my description of the religious church lines up with God's assessment, we are in big trouble. When His people have been out of line in the past, He has brought judgment on them. What will God's response be? Will He shake the church?

The most common use of the verb *to shake* is what you do to someone who is deep asleep and has not been roused by gentler means! They need shaking to wake them up.

Vulcanologists can predict when a big volcanic eruption is about to take place by the early, smaller tremors. These are preliminary shakings that precede the real event. Do you see where I am going with these examples?

Do you ever wonder if God will shake the Church? To wake it up from its stupor. Have a look at some of the scriptures below and see if you think He has already shaken Israel and the Church.

> For the LORD shall smite Israel, as a reed is shaken in the water, and he shall root up Israel out of this good land, which he gave to their fathers, and shall scatter them beyond the river, because they have made their groves, provoking the LORD to anger. (1Kings 14:15).

> Then the earth shook and trembled; and the foundations of the mountains shook; they trembled because he was angry. (Psalm 18:7).

> You have rejected us, O God, and burst forth upon us; you have been angry—now restore us! You have shaken the land and torn it open; mend its fractures for it is quaking. You have shown your people desperate times; you have given us wine that makes us stagger. (Psalm 60).

> In that day men will throw away to the rodents and bats their idols of silver and gold which they made to worship. They will flee to caverns in the rocks and to the overhanging crags from dread of the Lord and the splendour of his majesty when he rises to shake the earth. (Isaiah 2:20-21).

Do you think God can do it again?

> And His voice shook the earth then, but now He has promised, saying, "Yet once more I will shake not only the earth, but also the heaven." This expression, "Yet once more," denotes the removing of those things which can be shaken, as of created things, so that those things which cannot be shaken may remain. (Hebrews 12:26-27).

> Immediately after the tribulation of those days the sun shall be darkened, and the moon shall not give her light, and the stars shall fall from heaven, and the powers of the heavens shall be shaken. (Matthew 24:29).

For argument's sake, let us suppose God is angry. In what form might his anger and shaking take? Might these shakings be simply the preliminary to the BIG shaking?

> Tidal waves—done that.
>
> Earthquakes and volcanoes—done that.
>
> Massive fires—done that.
>
> Floods—done that.

Catastrophic weather—done that.

Wars and invasions—done that.

Famine—done that.

Radioactive contamination—done that.

Plagues—done that.

Massive displacement of people—done that.

Civil disorder, rejection of authority and riots—done that.

Global warming—you be the judge.

The end times described in Revelation tell how God sends one disaster after another, giving people the opportunity to repent. They haven't and they don't—even after everything that is happening.

Why would God be so angry as to bring disaster on us? Go on, have a guess. Let's start with the ten commandments.

1. You will have no other gods. *We worship money, power, and status.*
2. No idols. *Hollywood. Sport heroes.*
3. Profanity against the name of God. *OMG. Normalization of swearing in the cinema.*
4. Observe the Sabbath. *Too busy. Sunday sport.*
5. Honour your father and mother. *Elder abuse.*
6. Don't murder. *Rampant. Abortion. Interracial violence. Domestic violence.*
7. Don't commit adultery. *Even more rampant. Rape. Date rape.*
8. Don't steal. *Everyone does. False tax returns.*
9. Don't lie. *Everyone does. Internet fraud. The post-truth era.*
10. Don't lust after someone else's wife. *Most men do.*

That was my tongue-in-cheek assessment of how we are doing in terms of keeping just the ten commandments. But Jesus raised the stakes even higher. He said we have sinned even by THINKING about killing or committing adultery. We are not doing well, are we?

But what God must be most upset about is the beating his Church has taken. In this short book, I have laid out some of the errors that I believe have perverted the Christian faith into a religion over the last 2000 years.

Yes, He is angry.

The spread of the COVID-19 virus has been provocative. It is interesting to see the different responses of various church groups. In January 2022, Hillsong in Sydney held a youth meeting with hundreds of young people in attendance, dancing and singing, all in contravention to the standing orders of the day. How bad an example is that? Some churches have folded and no longer exist. Yet others are holding various versions of the Sunday service on Skype or Zoom. The pandemic has been a great example where people have appeared lost without the Sunday service. In reality, the *ekklesia* has not been closed at all because it cannot be confined to a building.

Yes, He has begun to shake what can be shaken, and yes, He will continue to shake what can be shaken. His history of longstanding forbearance with Israel suggests He will give us time to repent, but if we do not wake up, He will eventually SHAKE us awake. Why? Because He longs for His bride, the Church (*ekklesia*), to be pure again.

REFLECTIONS

What is God using to shake His Church today? is Church? Is God demanding our attention by allowing, for instance, COVID-19 to spread throughout the world? Or the impending catastrophe following global warming caused by mankind's mismanagement of His created world?

Is God wanting a more profound response than just reorganizing the services online instead of face-to-face? Or limiting the number of masked attendees? Is He asking us to rethink "church" more radically than that?

When God finally put an end to temple worship and animal sacrifice, He allowed the Romans to destroy the temple completely in 70AD. Is God now in the process of closing down the religious, hierarchical versions of church today?

16

CALLED OUT OF WHAT?

I have mentioned in the chapter on the *ekklesia* how we are the "called-out ones." But what are we called out of? As we might expect, the Old Testament gives us a foreshadowing of the answer. As early as the book of Exodus, God called Israel out of Egypt. In his book *The Church in the Wilderness*, Chip Brogden describes four events when God's people are called out.[15] Let us go through them.

Egypt

First, the Israelites were called out of Egypt. Under the leadership of Moses, the book of Exodus tells the story of the *ekklesia* escaping into the wilderness and onward to the Promised Land. God blessed them with food in the form of manna and quail along with providing them with water for the journey. But of course, the Israelites made a mess of the whole thing (starting with Moses). They became resentful and rebellious, even talking of going back to the bad conditions they left in Egypt rather than pressing on to the Promised Land. God would not let that rebellious generation reach the Promised Land, but the younger generation made it. In this story, the symbolism is not hard to spot—Egypt, Sodom and Babylon all represent the world, while Pharaoh represents Satan.

---

15 The Church in the Wilderness. Chip Brogden. The School of Christ. www.TheSchoolof-Christ.org

Babylon

No sooner had they entered the Promised Land than the Israelites began to backslide. Despite a series of prophets calling them back to the Word of God and the holy covenants, they persisted in their ways. There were occasional godly kings and periods of repentance and revival. But eventually God sent Nebuchadnezzar to destroy Israel. After 70 years in captivity, the Israelites were called out of Babylon. Only a handful of those transported to Babylon chose to return to Jerusalem and rebuild the temple. Out of 1 million Jews in slavery in Babylon, only 42,000 returned.

Judaism

Having rebuilt the temple and settled again into the Promised Land, the Jews slipped back into idolatry and their own religious system. The priesthood was obsessed with outward appearance and the letter of the Law while disregarding mercy, grace, righteousness, faith and love. First it was John the Baptist who called the Jews to repentance, and then Jesus called out Jews from the structure of Judaism. He was sent specifically to the Jews and indeed forbade his disciples from preaching to the Gentiles. It was only after Jesus' death that Peter and then Paul began ministering to the Gentiles. Jesus reacted with vehemence and passion to the abuse of the temple court for money-changing, and He spoke strongly against the Pharisees and Sadducees who wanted the best seats and best robes. He was calling the *ekklesia* out of their religious ways, developed over hundreds of years where multiple rules governing behaviour had been invented and had to be obeyed. That was no more a success than reforming the Jews in earlier callouts! While a handful of Jews and Gentiles became believers, Jews for the most part stuck to Judaism. Nothing new there, then.

Catholicism

We next come to a prolonged period of darkness—the Dark Ages—when the light of Christ was nearly extinguished. The Roman Church had dominated Christianity since the fourth century, not allowing the laity access to the Bible and imposing priestly domination over every aspect of church life. Services were in Latin, so the public had no idea what the mass was about unless it was explained by the clergy.

Although the Eastern Roman State based in Constantinople (Byzantium) persevered for many hundreds of years more, the Western Roman State based in Rome withered. Their control over various parts of Europe was threatened, and invasion by previously held peoples and territory began. The suppression of the gospel by the Church together with political instability resulted in the Dark Ages that lasted up to 1500AD. While there had been murmurings of revolt against the rigid Roman Church before, the appearance of Luther in 1517 began the actual revolution. His message was primarily the objection to allowing "indulgences," paying money to the church for the forgiveness of sins. But he unleashed far more than that. Sensing freedom from the Pope, protesters (Protestants) began a massive breakaway—the Reformation had begun. Christians were being called out from the Roman Church, the fourth callout. Once more, the majority of Roman Catholics stayed in that church, and today it remains the largest denomination in Christianity in the world.

Each time God calls His people out, there is the physical aspect such as travelling through the wilderness, but also a spiritual side as well. God is always calling His people to a closer walk with Him, calling them out of the world. But the leaving is often hard. Many believe in the axiom, "Better the hardship you know than the unknown hardship ahead." However, God's people must accept that the journey may not be easy.

> "Come out of Babylon, my people, in case you take part in her sins, in case you share in her plagues." (Revelation 18:4).

Is that the last callout, or is there still another? Yes, there is another! I believe that God is calling Christians out of the present-day hierarchical, organized, religious church system, whether that is the Roman Catholic Church or one of the many Protestant post-Reformation churches. This will be too difficult for most. Are all Protestant churches hierarchical? I am sure some strive to avoid this pitfall. Let me not be the judge of which is hierarchical, and which is not.

REFLECTIONS

Is your church hierarchical with a division between the laity and the clergy?

Are you being called out from where you are in your church? If so, are you prepared to pay the price?

Is it possible God is asking you to stay put and make a difference in the situation you find yourself? Or is that just the easy option?

17

THE FAITHFUL REMNANT

The simple, unadorned gospel has survived outside of the main religious churches. It has survived in a few places with a few individuals, with a remnant. The Old Testament refers to the remnant in many places (e.g., Isaiah 6:13, 10:20-23, Jeremiah 39 and 40), and the New Testament returns to this image in Romans 11.

A remnant is a tailor's term. Imagine a large table with a bolt of cloth laid out and a tailor cutting the pattern of a dress from it. When he comes to a tricky bit, he will cut a fragment off, and it will fall to the floor and will not be used in the dress. By evening there will be lots of off-cuts or remnants lying on the floor from different patterns of cloth that he will collect up. These remnants are not useful to make an attractive bit of clothing, but he may decide to sew them together and make a patchwork garment which he can sell cheaply. The result would be considered of low value and not useful.

I like this image of the faithful remnant: I envision a group of believers who are cut off from the main body of believers and who are not considered worthy of respect, but perhaps even regarded with suspicion. Consequently, they may be swept up and discarded. But they have nonetheless been cut from the same bolts of fine cloth. So many faithful remnants have been cast aside by the mainline churches since the first century. But they have not been deterred from practicing what they have believed to be the unadorned gospel.

"Then Elijah said to them, 'I am the only one of the Lord's prophets left, but Baal has four hundred and fifty prophets' " (1Kings 18:22). Elijah was convinced that he was the only one left who worshiped the one true God. He was wrong. He repeated his cry of despair in 1Kings 19:14 when he said: "I am the only one left and they are trying to kill me." But God smiled (maybe?) and said, "Yet I reserve seven thousand in Israel—all whose knees have not bowed down to Baal and all whose mouths have not kissed him" (1Kings 19:18). God had a remnant. God always has a remnant.

So often through history, it seems that the entire *ekklesia* has lost its way and is enveloped in the church religious system. Not so. By examining records, we find that there have always been remnants running throughout the history of Christianity, groups who have separated themselves from the mainstream churches and tried to practice first century Christianity. Sometimes they have worshiped quietly in remote locations, no apparent threat to anyone. At other times they have been on a collision course with the mainstream church. Let us look at a few examples.

Three characters stand out in Europe—Patrick, Columba and Aiden.

Patrick (?385-461?). Born in Roman Britain, Patrick was captured by a group of Irish pirates at the age of sixteen. They took him to Ireland where he was enslaved and held captive for six years. During his captivity he converted to Christianity. He escaped back to England where Patrick continued to study Christianity. He studied in Europe but then returned to Ireland as a Christian missionary. He trained missionaries and sent them to many parts of the known world.

Columba (521-597AD) was an Irish abbot and missionary evangelist. He studied under some of Ireland's most prominent church figures and founded several monasteries in the country. Around 563AD he and his twelve companions crossed to Scotland, settling in Iona, then part of the Ulster kingdom of Dál Riata. He used the abbey as a base for spreading Celtic Christianity among the pagan north. Iona became a remarkable centre of learning and evangelism that has made it famous for evermore. The Iona missionaries pioneered the gospel among the Picts of Caledonia and the Saxons of England. Iona was a missionary centre for 641 years until it was destroyed by the Benedictine monks.

Aiden (died 651AD), a Celtic missionary educated at Iona's university, pioneered the gospel work among the English. He established a centre of learning on the isle of Lindisfarne on the eastern coast of Northern England and modelled it on the Iona plan. It was Celtic missionaries who won two-thirds of the English population to the Christian faith.

In 664AD the Papacy produced a crisis in the Celtic Church. In the Council of Whitby, the Celtic and Roman churches debated over the question of the true Easter. The king of Northumbria sided with the Catholics, an action which had a deleterious effect on the Celtic Church. The later invasion of the Danes in 820AD checked the spread of Catholicism; however, it also devastated the English Celtic churches right to the Welsh and Scottish borders. Finally, in 1066AD through the agency of William the Conqueror, a Roman Catholic instrument, the Papacy gained dominance in England.

Yet as late as 1058AD the Celtic Church was still independent and in the main, in harmony with the teachings of the Iona founders. In 1130AD, a final blow fell when the Scottish Celtic clergy were dispossessed of their lands and expelled from their parishes. However, among many of the congregations the biblical teachings of Iona continued, albeit underground, later nurtured by Waldensian and Wycliffe missionaries. Thankfully, the faith of Iona continued to flower.

The faith represented by the Celtic leaders remained powerful in Scotland, Ireland, Wales, and in the southwestern part of England. Followers of the truth persisted down through the centuries, so that when John Wycliffe began his revival centuries later, his followers are thought by some to have been those who had maintained from generation to generation the faith of Aiden.

In India, many Christian communities existed by 500AD, mainly because India had become a haven for persecuted Christians. Numerous

Christians had fled from persecution within the Roman Empire eastward to Persia and had subsequently fled to India. But persecution followed them into the Persian lands. In 1500AD, when the Catholic Portuguese arrived in India, the Jesuits followed, and the true church was soon crushed.

English Dissenters were Protestants who separated from the Church of England in the 17th and 18th centuries. They opposed state interference with religious matters and founded their own churches. They played a pivotal role in the spiritual development of the United States. They flourished briefly during the Protectorate of Oliver Cromwell who said, “no bishop, no king”. After the restoration of the monarchy in 1660, bishops were re-installed and the rights of the Dissenters were limited. Anglican clergy had to be ordained, but many withdrew from the state church. Other dissenter groups included Anabaptists, Puritans, and Quakers.

This story of the faithful remnant has been unfolding in parallel with the story of the main church movements—but is rarely told. I tell a brief version here to illustrate that some amazing men and women have gone before, clinging on to what they have believed is the simple, unadorned gospel, many dying for their belief. Their faith is a shining example of courage and persistence, one that bears copying. If we identify with them in any way, we should not be ashamed, but be honoured to walk the path they have trodden. The good news is that the remnant makes it in the end—Isaiah describes the remnant as stumps of terebinth and oak trees that have been cut down, leaving only the stumps above ground (Isaiah 6:13). But he then describes them as a holy seed. Job explains in 14:7: “At least there is hope for a tree; if it is cut down it will sprout again.....yet at the scent of water it will bud.”

REFLECTIONS

Has there always been a faithful remnant? Yes.

Will there always be a faithful remnant? Yes.

Is it fun being a faithful remnant? Not really. You will be persecuted, bad-mouthed by men and refined by God.

18

THE CHURCH AT ANTIOCH

If the religious church veered off course as this book claims, what did it look like before the changes happened? The *ekklesia* at Antioch gives us one glimpse.

Antioch (present-day Antakya in Southern Turkey) was founded by the Greeks in the fourth century BC at the crossroads of major trade routes. Later, Rome took the city over and made it the capital of the Province of Syria. It became the Roman Empire's third most populous and important city behind Rome and Alexandria. It lay about 300 miles north of Jerusalem.

Why is Antioch of interest to us in this book? Because the first Gentile church was founded at Antioch. Examining the dynamics of this church gives us a clear insight into the purest form of congregation/church/*ekklesia* that we have from the earliest period in Christianity. The church founders had to contend with opposition and competition. But they were a dynamic group who overcame these obstacles successfully. A reading of the Acts of the Apostles quickly reveals that the *ekklesia* at Antioch played a crucial role in establishing Christianity. With its mixture of Jews and Gentiles, the city became fertile ground for the growth and spread of the faith and was a model congregation. The details of this story bear telling.

After the killing of Steven and subsequent persecution by the Romans, the followers of Jesus (not yet called Christians) scattered.

Some ended up in Antioch, not very far from Jerusalem, but in a different Roman Province. Scripture does not explain whether the climate toward Christians was different in Antioch, but one can guess that persecution followed them. As such, the followers would have had to be discreet and not make themselves stand out. There were clearly enough followers in the city for it to become known in the surrounding area, and it became a magnet. Followers from other locations came to Antioch to preach and disciple. Word within the believers spread, and news reached the ears of those in Jerusalem. They dispatched Barnabas to Antioch to head up the initiative (Acts 11:19-26). He in turn recruited Paul, who was only a short distance away in Tarsus. In addition to the assembly of evangelists in the city was an assortment of faiths and races. Jews were prominent and became a target for the preachers. Greeks in the city there became a target later. In contrast, there was a strong flavour of pagan worship with all the usual Greek and Roman gods. This was the melting pot that was Antioch in the first century AD.

Some of the special characteristics of the *ekklesia* in Antioch were:

The first Gentile ekklesia. Initially the dispersed believers preached only to the Jews (Acts 11:19-21) Soon, however, men from Cyprus and Cyrene went to Antioch and preached to the Greeks as well. James, a ruling elder in Jerusalem, reinforced the acceptance of Gentiles, stating they should not have to live by Jewish laws to be saved. James also laid out some practical guidelines and solutions for fellowship between Jews and Gentiles. A letter of encouragement was drawn up by the council, and Judas and Silas were appointed as official delegates to deliver the correspondence to the church at Antioch. The letter stipulated only four requirements of new converts, that they should abstain from food sacrifice to idols, from blood, from the meat of strangled animals, and from sexual immorality (Acts 15:23-29).

Sound teaching. The teaching, preaching and evangelism were clearly very successful. Luke reports, "The Lord's hand was with them, and a great number of people believed and turned to the Lord" (Acts 11:21). With so many converts, it is surprising the *ekklesia* did not attract more attention from the Romans who were persecuting Christians in other parts of the Empire. If they did, we are not told about it in scripture.

Conflict management. Like any other group of humans, the *ekklesia* at Antioch experienced conflict and controversy. However, they were adept at addressing conflict when it arose, were able to bring it to resolution, and were able to move on when resolution was reached. Some Judean Christians of a Pharisaic background began teaching the believers that circumcision was required of Gentiles for salvation. Paul disagreed. He and Barnabas were appointed by the church at Antioch to represent the Gentile Christians at a meeting of leaders in Jerusalem. Paul and Barnabas convinced them that circumcision was not needed; rather, they believed it was through the grace of Jesus that they were saved (Acts 15:7-11).

Missionary focus. The city's location at a chief trade intersection between Egypt, Asia Minor, Greece, Italy, and Mesopotamia made the church at Antioch a strategic hub for spreading the gospel to cities around the Mediterranean and beyond. The church at Antioch was the launching site for several of Paul's missionary journeys. In many cases, the church at Antioch commissioned the missionaries for a specific task. Paul also made Antioch his base between journeys.

Doctrine. Antioch was where Paul disputed with Peter over his segregation of Gentile believers during mealtimes. Paul called Peter's actions "hypocrisy," and blamed him for leading other Jewish believers astray (Galatians 2:13-14).

Leadership. There was no single evangelist or apostle who could claim to be in charge or take the credit for the growth of the *ekklesia*. Acts mentions several individuals who contributed to leadership at this time:

Barnabas, Paul, Silas, Agabus, Lukus, Judas, Simeon and Manaen. It was acknowledged that the Holy Spirit was the prime mover in all things.

Generosity. In Antioch, Agabus predicted a severe famine that would strike the entire Roman world. The *ekklesia* at Antioch responded swiftly and eagerly by preparing a generous offering to aid the Jerusalem church whenever the famine hit. They entrusted their gift to Barnabas and Paul, who carried it back to the elders of the church in Jerusalem (Acts 11:27-30).

Open to change. Things must have changed quickly in Antioch. They had no model to follow, but just the Holy Spirit to guide them. They must have preached in a way they had never preached before to an audience who had never been preached to before. They had simultaneous challenges of building a community, a teaching ministry, a mission ministry, and always with the focus on fulfilling the mission to usher in the Kingdom of God.

We are not told in Acts how long the church at Antioch functioned. We know that there were many church plants subsequently in Asia Minor and throughout the world. And we are told that for years Paul used it as his base. But whether its form and function lasted for long is not clear. We know that other churches in Asia Minor suffered change for the worse. They must have done something right in Antioch as it can reasonably be called the cradle of Christendom.

REFLECTIONS

If Antioch was the model church plant, is it the only model God wants us to follow?

How does culture influence how we plant new ekklesia*?*

Is your church similar to the Antioch ekklesia*? If not, what does it lack?*

19

THE HOUSE CHURCH

The previous chapter described the highly successful *ekklesia* at Antioch. Has there been any other effort to experiment with Christian meetings that did not include "going to church"? Of course. In fact, "going to church" is a relatively recent experience. By recent, I mean since 300AD! As I mention in Chapter 5 on the Temple, Roman Emperor Constantine provided pagan temples for worship on a Sunday. The temples became instant churches.

But Christianity did not start with Sunday morning services at church. As well as the meeting of the *ekklesia* at Antioch, there are other descriptions of early church life in the New Testament where groups regularly met together and where believers were close-knit, dynamic, and excited about their faith. These meetings were in people's homes where they experienced close friendship.

> "Every day they devoted themselves to meeting together in the temple area and to breaking bread in their homes" (Acts 2:46a).

> "When he [Peter] realized this, he went to the house of Mary, the mother of John who is called Mark, where there were many people gathered in prayer" (Acts 12:12)

> "When they [Paul and Silas] had come out of the prison, they went to Lydia's house where they saw and encouraged

> the brothers, and then they left" (Acts 16:40).
>
> "Greet Priscilla and Aquila, my co-workers in Christ Jesus...greet also the church at their house" (Romans 16:3,5).
>
> "Give greetings to the brothers in Laodicea and to Nympha and to the church in her house" (Colossians 4:15).
>
> "Paul, a prisoner for Christ Jesus, and Timothy our brother, to Philemon, our beloved and our co-worker, to Apphia our sister, to Archippus our fellow soldier, and to the church at your house" (Philemon v1-2).

Note in these examples how often the women are the ones opening their homes for believers.

The discussion on *koinonia* could have come in a number of places in this book, but let's deal with it here. *Koinonia* (κοινονια) is a Greek word meaning fellowship, a close mutual relationship, participation, sharing. Humans seem to have a universal need for *koinonia*, belonging to a group where they feel loved and respected. Satan's perverted version of *koinonia* would be the underworld gangs where young men and women get enticed into gangs because the world they live in has not accepted them. Gangs make them feel they belong. Of course, once in a gang, it is very difficult to get out alive. Others turn to more healthy expressions such as societies, sports fan clubs, golf clubs and many more. There is nothing wrong with such fellowships unless they become a substitute for the meaningful relationship that is possible with other Christians. *Koinonia* should be the glue that holds the *ekklesia* together. Men and women should feel unconditionally loved and respected in the *ekklesia*.

We must ask in what Christian environment is *koinonia* best developed? Is shaking hands with the vicar on the way out of church *koinonia*? I don't think so! If you want to impress the person you think you want to marry, will a quick handshake do it? I don't think so! You must spend time with that individual and hear their heart. There are many ways one might develop *koinonia*, and house church is certainly one of them. It meets such a deep need in our humanity. It is a vital tool towards honouring the second commandment of loving our neighbour.

Initially the motivation to meet in homes would have been expediency. In other words, it was the obvious choice, the alternative being somewhere outdoors or in secret such as in a cave. Until Roman persecution ended, Christians had to be wary about where and how they met, so did not want their meetings to draw attention to themselves. There followed a long period when Western Christians were largely free of persecution, allowing an openness in location of worship. This has generally meant Sunday worship in church.

Despite persecution (or was it because of persecution?) during the first 300 years of the church age, the numbers grew rapidly. Is this dynamic consigned to history? By no means! Let us look at China. In the mid-nineteenth century, European missionaries flooded into China. Although they made considerable progress in converting the local population, the presence of the white "colonial" missionaries was seen by the Chinese as part of the attempt by outsiders to dominate China. Indeed, other appalling aspects of interference by European powers were linked in the minds of the Chinese to the missionaries. Economic pressures resulted in the Opium Wars where large quantities of opium were forced onto the local population, many of whom became addicted. This is part of the backstory of why Christianity in China today is condemned by the ruling party. Although initially suppressed, Christianity has flourished under persecution. For the same reasons affecting early Christians, the believers were driven underground. Many have been martyred,[16] while others have endured long prison sentences. Bibles have had to be hidden. And yet thousands of Christians are continuing to meet in homes (underground)

---

[16] One source claims that around 27 million people died as martyrs. Lawrence C, The Church in China: How It Survives and Prospers Under Communism. (Minneapolis: Bethany House Publishers, 1985).

throughout China, hearing the gospel from leaders who have not been ordained by any organisation.[17]

The underground *ekklesia* in China is a shining example of how house churches work. Clearly there would have to be some level of cultural adaptation for them to work in other countries. But the concept is dynamic, simple, and transferable.

The idea of a house church is not new to the West. Many churches have been running versions of house churches for years. But here is the rub. Churches have organised and supervised the start-up and content of the house churches under them. The house churches tend to orbit around mother churches, depending on them for membership, teaching content, and even location. Most importantly they come under the authority of the mother church leaders. They are, in effect, babies of the parent religious system.

I have indicated above some of my reservations about house churches. But I am a great fan of them, nonetheless. It is in this environment that true, meaningful, supportive relationships (*koinonia*) are built. It is also a place where interactive learning can take place. One person may lead the teaching, but because of the intimate setting, others can ask questions or express a different point of view from the teacher without fear of ridicule or censorship. Such interactions are generally impossible in the ordinary Sunday service in church where the congregation is normally passive and, at most, would be encouraged to clap at some major statement the preacher makes.

I am also a great fan of food as an evangelistic tool! There is something intimate about sharing a meal with friends and family. It has always been so. Providing nibbles or even a sit-down meal is a wonderful component of a house church meeting. I have participated and even led house churches for forty years and have been mightily blessed by them.

---

[17] The exact number of Christians in China is uncertain. Winter suggests that Christians have grown from one or two million to easily 50 million currently. Ralph D. Winter, "About You," (Pasadena, CA: U.S. Center for World Mission, 1983.

So how can a house church start up if it is not to be a satellite of a mother church? An individual can simply invite round some of his/her neighbours and see what the Holy Spirit does. Or we may choose to have a group of men only or women only. The choice of attendees may dictate the time the meeting is held. Without resorting to sexual stereotypes, mums or house fathers can often meet during the day, whereas a working partner may be limited to evenings. So long as we allow the Holy Spirit to lead, it will be great.

It is important that any house church has a connection with other Christians. Otherwise, there is the danger of cult formation or other forms of wrong teaching. I believe the house church is the building block of the *ekklesia*. And there should be some links with other house churches. Revelation 2-3 describes Jesus speaking to churches in Asia Minor. He talks about the church (*ekklesia*) in Ephesus, for example. I do not think there was only one house church there constituting the "church of Ephesus." There were surely many. But they were known collectively as the church at Ephesus. I imagine they had appointed elders for the city church. And there would have been those with an apostolic gifting who perhaps toured the known house churches to encourage them and offer direction to the teaching.

London, a metropolis, is made up of many boroughs. Melbourne, another metropolis, is made up of multiple cities. Each large city has its own method of dividing the city into manageable administrative entities. I believe these entities should all consider themselves as part of "the church in the city of...." and appoint elders and deacons accordingly. Each house church should relate to their respective city elders. We should expect that the fivefold ministry will be present in each city as well. The structure I am describing is not hierarchical but flat. The elders are not in charge. They are servant leaders. The Holy Spirit must be given leadership.

I have dealt with deconstructing the temple in another chapter. The church building as we know it has little place in the deconstructed church. It does make sense, however, to have a central office in each city. In this office, there can be meeting rooms and even seminar rooms. It can perform various administrative functions for the whole city. However, this is a far cry from "the church building."

REFLECTIONS

How would Christianity flourish in your city if there was no church building? How would people react—perplexed, angry, enthusiastic?

How might you start a house church in your neighbourhood?

If there was a groundswell of desire to have a big gathering to worship together, could a large hall be hired for the occasion?

20

WOMEN IN MINISTRY

Having seen how women played such an important part in the early house church, I want to include a section on women in the *ekklesia* today. To leave the female gender out of a discussion would be missing half of the *ekklesia*. I feel strongly that women have been given a poor deal in Christian theology.

There were many women mentioned in the Old Testament. Women such as Miriam prophesied (Genesis 15), there were female judges such as Deborah (Judges 4), Esther saved the Jewish race from persecution, Ruth was the outsider who would be the progenitor of Jesus, and we are told of the legendary wife of noble character (Proverbs 31:10). Nevertheless, women at that time and in that culture were expected to be the homemaker and produce babies.

Jesus, too, was brought up in a male-dominated society. His father had the traditional role of bread winner as carpenter, and Mary had babies. But Mary was clearly not entirely a stay-at-home mum. She appears in the New Testament in various locations—the Passover feast at Jerusalem, the marriage ceremony in Cana (John 2), and at the cross on the day of the Crucifixion.

The inner circle of twelve disciples were male, but there must have been several women in the group following Jesus. We know about Mary Magdalene, Martha and her sister Mary of Bethany. And we know Jesus taught an audience of both men and women (and probably children). What is interesting is that Jesus never distinguished between genders when teaching. Whatever he taught was as applicable to the woman as to the man. He did not forbid any activity specifically related to women, and he healed both men and women. Given the cultural conditions in Israel at the time, this approach was indeed radical and was surely a pointer to women's future role.

Paul understood the interdependence of man and woman. "In the Lord, however, woman is not independent of man, nor is man independent of woman. For as woman came from man, so also man is born of woman" (1Corinthians 11:11). Paul goes on to describe spiritual gifts and does not stipulate gender (1Corinthians 12:1). He also describes the fivefold ministry of apostle, prophet, pastor, evangelist, and teacher. Again, he does not stipulate gender (Ephesians 4:10). I take from this that both men and women can be gifted as apostles, prophets, evangelists, pastors and teachers.

Part of Paul's teaching is confusing. He says that women should not speak in church (1 Corinthians 14:34). "In the church" here is from the Greek "*en pasais tais ekklaisias,*" literally in all the assemblies. Consequently, this would include anywhere where Christians gathered. This seems to be contradicted by accepting that women may prophecy and teach.

Again, Paul limits the role of women when he teaches on marriage. "Submit to one another out of reverence to Christ. Wives, submit to your husbands as to the Lord. For the husband is the head of the wife as Christ is head of the church, his body of which he is the Savior. Now as the church submits to Christ, so all wives should submit to their husbands in everything. Husbands, love your wives, just as Christ loved the church and gave himself up for her to make her holy, cleansing her by the washing with water through the word, and to present her to himself as a radiant church, without stain or wrinkle or any other blemish, but holy and blameless. In this way, husbands ought to love their wives as their own bodies." (Ephesians 5:21). I especially like the part where the husband is the head of the wife just as Christ is head of the church—in other words he must be prepared to die to protect his wife, just as Jesus was prepared to die to protect his *ekklesia*. That part of marriage is not often stressed!

When discussing these misogynist passages, I don't like resorting to the catch-all explanation that Paul was only referring to a specific culture and that it does not apply to any other culture. Even worse, I do not want to say he was wrong. But I just don't get it. There are those who counter these passages, however. It has been suggested by experts in literary critique that Paul did not write all the letters attributed to him. And it is possible that the passages I find so confusing were added by someone who thought they knew better some years later. I like that explanation but have no skills to verify or dispute such statements.

While I deeply respect those who choose to live cloistered lives of contemplation and prayer or those who lead lives of dedicated service to the poor, it saddens me to know they may be required to be celibate and wear garments that shout "clergy." Why should a good person committed to good works be burdened with unbiblical rules? Can a married woman with children not equally lead a life of service?

If you agree that the scriptures allow for a woman to be part of the fivefold ministry, how is she expected to fulfill her calling when she is banned from teaching or even speaking in the *ekklesia* (but allowed to teach in children's Sunday school). I prefer to admit I do not have the full understanding of the teachings attributed to Paul. My chapter on the priesthood has already made it clear that women are royal priests to the same extent as males, simply by being believers. I just don't understand how Paul (or comments attributed to him) can cast such a diminutive and subservient role on the woman. I prefer to emphasize the teaching of Jesus which was gender neutral. I find it incomprehensible that a loving God should create inequality between genders. Certainly, He gave us different strengths, but not all women have the same strengths just as not all men have the same strengths. And I am convinced that God loves us all equally. If you are a woman reading this, may I encourage you to pursue with all your heart whatever you feel God is calling you to do in your *ekklesia*?

REFLECTIONS

Can a woman be a priest? Is she not already a royal priest simply by being a believer?

Can a woman be ordained? Is she not already a royal priest if she is a believer, so why would she become ordained as well?

Can a woman be an apostle, prophet, pastor, evangelist, or teacher? I see no prohibition in scripture.

Can a woman be an elder or deacon?

21

THE LORD'S SUPPER

I have identified elements of the religious church that I propose to pull down or deconstruct, there are others that are clearly essential to keep. The Lord's Supper is definitely one to keep.

I have included the Lord's Supper or Holy Communion in this short book because it features as a significant part of today's Christianity and deserves similar scrutiny to other elements I have discussed elsewhere in the book. It is also called the Eucharist, derived from the Greek word meaning grateful. How did it get into today's practices? And is it biblical?

At least, it is not derived from anything pagan. Hooray!

In fact, the Lord's Supper is derived from the Jewish custom of breaking bread as a family at the start of the Sabbath, i.e., after 6pm on Friday evening. It is a lovely intimate ceremony that every Jewish father will lead at the start of the Sabbath family meal. The Jewish day of rest, or Shabbat in Hebrew, begins on Friday at sundown and ends on Saturday at nightfall. Shabbat dinners may consist of bread, fish, soup, meat (especially lamb) or poultry, side dishes, and dessert.

Jesus gathered his disciples together for the meal known as "The Last Supper." This was not on a Friday; it was in fact after 6pm on a Wednesday as they were entering the Feast of Passover and the Feast of Unleavened Bread. There were thirteen at table including Jesus and Judas. Jesus took the bread and broke it, and gave it to his disciples, saying, "Take and eat; this is my body given for you; do this in remembrance of me. (Luke 22:19)." Then he took the cup, gave thanks, and offered it to them saying "Drink from it, all of you. This is my blood of the new covenant which is poured out for many for the forgiveness of sins." (Matthew 26:26-28).

Clearly, the Christian custom to celebrate the Lord's Supper comes from the Jewish Shabbat ceremony. Jesus did not change the actions but revealed a new meaning to the ceremony. It would no longer just commemorate the escape from Egypt, but now would commemorate his sacrificial death on the cross.

The two main elements are the bread and the wine. The Old Testament describes the Feast of Passover and the Feast of Unleavened Bread (the bread must be unleavened i.e., with no yeast, symbolic of no sin) (Exodus 12). We can assume that Jesus offered the bread to his disciples as unleavened bread. Christian churches vary in offering leavened or unleavened bread (usually in the form of a cracker) to communicants. Personally, I like a nice fresh baguette!

The wine is offered either from a large communal chalice or in individual thimbles. Again, churches vary, some offering alcoholic wine while others offer fruit juice. The fruit juice is offered out of respect to those who may have an addiction problem to alcohol. So long as the bread and wine are offered to honour the Lord, I believe either form is acceptable to Him.

Is there anything contentious about the Lord's Supper? In one word—"transubstantiation." The Catholic Church practices that the bread and the wine are transformed into the real blood and real body of Christ because of the prayer of the priest, and communicants eat the real body and drink the real blood of Jesus. This means that Jesus must be resurrected and crucified all over again at each service. In fact, the Bible confirms that Jesus' sacrificial death on the cross was a once-and-for-all event that is sufficient to wipe away the sins of all who believe in him. Let us not crucify him repeatedly.

If there can be any doubt about this interpretation, we need to go back to the original text. Jesus gave his disciples bread and wine. They were NOT part of his actual body. His blood had not yet been spilt; his body had not yet been broken. The bread and wine were SYMBOLIC of his sacrifice that was about to happen in a few hours.[18]

Most Christians who have been accustomed to attending church services will be familiar with the solemnity and ritual around the Lord's Supper. Jesus was prefacing the Seder meal with his announcements about the new commemorative aspect of the bread and the wine and about the new covenant that was being inaugurated before their eyes. It was NOT a solemn occasion, it did not require special robes, and it was full of anticipation of the traditional meal to follow.

One of my greatest joys as an elder has been to administer the bread and the wine to the members of the community. I had no pre-rehearsed words to say but would speak as the Lord led. Sometimes He would give me a special word of encouragement for an individual which as often as not would transform their faces into surprise and joy. Wherever and however we choose to hold an *ekklesia*, it is such a privilege to be able to share the meal with fellow believers, being thankful and remembering that Jesus died for us on the cross.

---

18 We should not be sceptical about the use of symbols in everyday speech. When you pay for groceries with a $20 bill, the shopkeeper does not say, "This is just a piece of paper, I don't accept it." He knows it is a symbol of the gold in the bank to that value. Even gold is a symbol of value if you think about it. Just because it looks shiny and is relatively rare, we attribute value to it. Don't get me started on Bitcoin.

REFLECTIONS

Do you need to be specially qualified to administer the bread and the wine?

Is it acceptable to commemorate Jesus' sacrifice on the cross by breaking bread and taking wine (or fruit juice) in private homes with no ordained minister present?

Do we need a special text for every time we celebrating the communion?

Does the bread and wine really *change into the real body and real blood of Christ after the priest blesses it?*

THE MATZO BREAD

This paragraph is out of context in that I have included it to provide readers with a sense of wonder in relation to the Last Supper and how God reveals his Savior in amazing ways in the Scriptures. The unleavened bread used in the Passover and during the Feast of the Unleavened Bread is called "*Matzo or Matzoh.*" Matzo has holes, stripes, and no yeast. The bread is placed in the middle section of a linen cloth with three pockets, the *Matzoh Tosh*. Now we can see why the middle *matzoh* is broken during the Passover, then hidden or buried. The three pockets represent the trinity Godhead. Jesus's body was broken for us, He died, and He was buried. But He didn't stay dead—He came back to life, came out of the tomb! That is represented by bringing out the *matzo* later in the ceremony. It is then broken into pieces and passed out to each person. And this is the exact moment during the Last Supper, when Jesus said, "This is my body which is broken for you." Jews have celebrated using the Matzo for centuries but have failed to associate it with Jesus, the risen Lord.

THE FOUR CUPS OF THE PASSOVER

The meal is slightly different at Passover. It is called the Seder and there are four wine cups during the meal (but only one in the weekly Friday evening meal). The four cups stand for the four "I will" statements that are recorded in Exodus 6:6-7. God revealed to Moses the plan by which He would redeem the children of Israel. In a prophetic sense, God was also revealing how He would redeem His elect to become His children. Based on the four promises in the passage above there are the four cups of the Passover feast:

- The Cup of Sanctification—based on God's statement, "I will bring you out from under the burdens of the Egyptians"
- The Cup of Deliverance—based on God's statement, "I will deliver you from slavery to them"
- The Cup of Redemption—based on God's statement, "I will redeem you with an outstretched arm"
- The Cup of Restoration—based on God's statement, "I will take you to be my people, and I will be your God".

"After supper he took the cup..." which would have been the cup of restoration. How prophetic is that? Wow!

22

BLOWN OFF COURSE

I like the analogy of a sailing boat blown off course and ending up on the rocks. In many ways, ALL denominations have been blown off course, as I suggested in Chapter 12. But some have deviated off course more than others, even though they may feel they represent the real gospel. Does a little deviation matter? And can a person be a real Christian if she/he worships in one of these denominations and espouses the denomination's specific beliefs? I believe there are many individuals within these denominations who accept Jesus as their Saviour and accept the Apostles' Creed. Does it matter if they are also going to confession with the priest? Or affirm Jehovah as the only name of God? I cannot answer such a question and have no intention of judging such persons. As individuals, we must all stand before the great white throne of judgment one day and answer for our own sins.

I do not want to write a long analysis of every denomination and how it has been blown off course. But the Roman Catholic Church represents such a large proportion of Christianity that I feel an urge to dissect some of the issues by which I consider it has been blown off course. This is really important as, from its very inception up until the Reformation, it dragged the majority of Christianity with it on what I consider to be its deviated course.

This is how Paul describes Jesus in Colossians 1:15. "Christ is the image of the invisible God, the firstborn over all creation. For by him all things were created, things in heaven and on earth, visible or invisible, whether thrones or powers or rulers or authorities; all things were created by him and for him... so that in everything he might have supremacy." If any person or system claims supremacy to match that of Jesus, he is satanic and has the spirit of the anti-Christ. Do you agree?

I will suggest that the Pope has in fact set himself as Christ's equal. And the Catholic Church has created and perpetuated a hierarchical system, set on maintaining the power of the pope and the gulf between the priesthood and the laity.

It is claimed by Catholics that Peter founded the church in Rome and that there has been unbroken succession from then on up to the present pope. Neither part of that sentence is true. It is doubtful whether Peter ever went to Rome. Paul was in Rome from 60-62AD and wrote letters from there. If Peter had been there, surely Paul would have mentioned it. Peter was not a great apostle – he failed Jesus on at least two occasions. Jesus made it clear that Peter left a lot to be desired in leadership. In Matthew 16:18, he describes Peter as a petros (little stone -πετρος) using a play on words with his name. He then said he would build his church not on a petros, but on a petra (πετρα), a bedrock. The bedrock Jesus is referring to in that verse is Peter's revelation that Jesus is the Christ, the Son of the living God mentioned earlier in verse 16. Jesus is the petra of the ekklesia. Paul had to rebuke Peter at one stage, making Peter less than ideal to be the next world leader!

Peter remained in Jerusalem after Pentecost but humbly described himself in 1 Peter 5:1 as a fellow elder, not the leader of the church, the leader in Jerusalem being James at the time. He went on to make more mistakes – the need for circumcision and the appointing of a replacement for Judas. The replacement twelfth apostle was probably Paul, not Matthias. Wrong again, Peter! Not the ideal candidate to found a world religion. Nor did Peter portray himself as such. In his letter 1 Peter 2;9, Peter describes the priesthood of all believers – he was not about to found a new church in Rome that promoted the exact opposite. The final nail in this particular coffin is that Peter was called to the Jews (Galatians 2;7-8), not the Gentiles (which was Paul's specific calling). It is stretching credibility beyond breaking point to accept that Peter was ever in Rome, that he founded the church in Rome, that Jesus gave him the mandate to be the founder of the entire post-Pentecostal church, and that he is now buried in the Vatican. Without Peter's line of succession, the Papal legitimacy crumbles.

A quick look at the papacy reveals that the first real pope was Gregory (590-604). This alone makes apostolic succession impossible. There were times throughout the history of the church when there was more than one person claiming to be the real pope at any one time. And there have been multiple times when there has been no pope at all. It was not until the First Vatican Council (1869-1870) in its decree Pastor Aeternus that the pope was voted infallible when he spoke 'ex Cathedra' ('from the Chair') on matters of faith and morals. Ludicrously, it was by a split vote! Now it has become impossible for the Pope to apologize for anything as he is caught in his own trap of infallibility. Apology would disprove his infallibility. No "bad behaviour" by the Catholic priesthood can ever be admitted, so forgiveness for past wrongs cannot be sought. A rather neat sidestep relies on the distinction between the sons and daughters of the church (the laity) and the priesthood. The priesthood can do no wrong, but the terrible actions carried out in the name of the church must have been perpetrated by the sons and daughters. This includes antisemitism, the crusades, and the Inquisition. When challenged about paedophilia by priests, the response has been that the incidence among priests was no higher than in the general population. No apology. No questioning whether forced celibacy was contributing to paedophilia. No sanctions by the church for the perpetrators.

One title for the pope is the Vicar of Rome. The word VICAR is derived from vicarious, in other words the pope is ruling vicariously on earth instead of Christ. He rules over his own kingdom – the Vatican – so he is beholden to no one. This is so wrong, because only Christ can be the head of the church on Earth. No one can criticise the pope on penalty of being cursed. He is unassailable and is the King of the World.

We cannot leave this discussion about Catholicism without expanding on its fixation with Mary, mother of Jesus. We know very little about Mary from the bible. We know that Jesus was conceived without sin (human sex), but we do not know if Mary ever sinned later in life. She certainly had other children (presumably by human sex), for example James and Jude. This makes her perpetual virginity as claimed by the Catholic Church somewhat unlikely! Likewise, there is no biblical support for her immaculate conception. We know she was at the wedding when Jesus turned water into wine. And we know she was at the cross when Jesus was crucified. How do we jump from these sparse details to discovering Mary is the primary intercessor between man and Jesus? There is a whole false theology around Mary to support her role in the Catholic Church. It accounts for the statue of Mary in almost every Catholic Church where she is worshipped. And it explains how she is invoked as a penance after the confessional box ("Hail Mary").

Peter Wagner[19] describes how the "Queen of Heaven" was a title given to several ancient sky goddesses worshipped throughout the ancient Mediterranean and Near East during ancient times. Goddesses known to have been referred to by this title include Inanna, Annat, Isis, Ishtar, Astarte and possibly Asherah. In Greco-Roman times Hera, and her Roman equivalent Juno bore this title.

Through her scheming and designing, Semiramis became the Babylonian "Queen of Heaven," and Nimrud, her son and consort, under various names, became the "divine son of heaven." Through the generations, in this idolatrous worship, Nimrud became the false Messiah, son of Baal the Sun-god. "Mother and Child" (Semiramis and Nimrud reborn) became chief objects of worship. This worship of "Mother and Child" spread over the world and was conveniently taken over by the church when Constantine shifted pagan practices into the

[19] *The queen's domain*, and *Confronting the queen of heaven*. Both by Peter Wagner

Christian church. In modern times, the title "Queen of Heaven" is still used by Catholics applying the ancient title to Mary, the mother of Jesus. It seems clear to me that the pagan goddess quietly morphed into a Mary. But she was not Mary, the mother of Jesus.

Catholics are taught that "Tradition" is of equal value to scripture in determining doctrine. Having invented such elements as purgatory and transubstantiation, the Catholic then announces them to be tradition and beyond questioning.

Here are some of the false doctrines that are contrary to scripture and perpetuated by the Catholic Church:

- A false priesthood, one that is the reverse of the priesthood of all believers.
- A false source of revelation – the teaching that scripture and Papal revelation and tradition are as valid as each other.
- A false promise for salvation, by faith AND works.
- Illegitimate power.
- Idolatrous worship of the saints.
- Veneration of angels.
- Exaltation of Mary above Jesus and God.
- Twisted sacrament of the mass – transubstantiation.
- False forgiveness of sins in the confessional.
- False forgiveness of sins for money – indulgencies.
- Invention of the teaching of purgatory.
- Worship of idols and relics.
- Prayers for the dead.
- Forced celibacy.
- The infallibility of the Pope.

Entire books have been written on why the Catholic Church is illegitimate and in apostasy. I have only skimmed the surface. There have always been men and women who have resisted the pope and Catholic doctrine and tradition. They have many times paid the ultimate price and been martyred (by the Catholic Church) for their belief.

REFLECTIONS

Can you be a Christian if you worship in a denomination that deviates significantly from scripture?

Are the teachings of Catholicism that are contrary to scripture inconsequential?

Is the focus on Mary a hangover from the pagan past? Does it matter that she is called the Queen of Heaven?

Is the Pope an exceptionally good man or an antichrist?

Do you think the Catholic Church invented hierarchical Christianity and then perpetuated it for 1700 years?

23

WHY DO PEOPLE GET PUT OFF BY THE GOSPEL?

How often do we send away to Amazon for an item and get told it comes with a free gift? We love free gifts. They are an integral part of the advertising economy. Would we ever refuse a free gift like that? I doubt it. But when God offers us a gift to pardon our sins and bring us into His eternal company, we say "No, thanks." Why?

Churchgoers ask why aren't people flocking to the church? I propose that this is the wrong question. It should be: "Why are more people not accepting the free gift of salvation and the forgiveness of sin offered through FAITH in Jesus Christ?"

The reasons people reject the gospel are too numerous to list in this short chapter. I have therefore selected a few of the more obvious. For many, the answer is that they reject the church and all it stands for, believing that faith in Jesus is inextricably bound up in having to enter the system of the religious church. The baby goes out with the bathwater! They think there must be a catch. And they certainly don't want to be made to go to church every Sunday like all those people they perceive as hypocrites. They know the past history of events perpetrated by the church in the name of Christianity—the Inquisition, the Crusades, burning heretics and more.

The reputation of the modern Christian Church with the wider public is also in tatters. Scandals continue to rock its image. They may be of a sexual nature such as the revelations about Ravi Zacharias. He had an amazing ministry of international speaking on every aspect of the faith but was found to have led a life of unfaithfulness to his wife. In addition, the news has focused much attention on the paedophilia of priests. Many a televangelist has had to resign after various scandals, especially of a financial nature. Others bring the gospel into disrepute through acquiring great riches. They flaunt their wealth with the purchase of private jets that "enable them to travel more easily." The public is appalled and rejects them, their ministry, and the gospel.

We have discussed disunity of the *ekklesia* already in Chapter 12 on denominations. The public also sees and hears about disunity among members of individual churches. Here the congregation will be polarised, often to the extent of a church split, with half leaving and going their own way. This is a terrible example to both fellow Christians and the wider public.

Some Christians are perceived as being Sunday-only Christians. In other words, their lives for six days a week are indistinguishable from the rest of the community. There is nothing so sure to cause the shout of "Humbug" as a disparity between the message and the way the carrier of the message lives. For instance, Elijah was told by God to act out his prophecies, thereby stopping such criticism. At one stage he had to strip off and go naked for three years (Isaiah 20:2-3). How many Sunday churchgoers blaspheme (Oh, my God!), drink to excess, flirt and commit adultery, or falsify their tax returns (steal)? Non-Christians notice.

Non-Christians hate to be judged. "You will end up in hell if you don't stop .... (*add your own word here*)." A sanctimonious Christian is likely to put anyone off church.

Western churchgoers are all too aware that most churches are failing in terms of numbers of attendees. However, this is not the case everywhere. In other parts of the world, South America, the Philippines, China, the church is expanding rapidly. People are hungry for the gospel. How the good news is offered and received in these growth countries is clearly different from its reception in the West.

Why are most congregations in the West composed of grey-haired people? Where is the youth? Perhaps the older generations have been too lax in their parenting, offering children the option of a spiritual education or not. Many young people have grown up in an environment completely lacking in any spirituality. It is not as if they have rejected spiritual things; rather, they simply have not seen a need to engage in that dimension of life. Suppressing and denying their innate spirituality have led them to an end-of-life situation where they have had no faith and no understanding of the afterlife. The result is society's fear of dying. It is the big unknown that must be fought against.

It is only natural for parents to allow children to choose in life. But too many young people have not been instructed about faith, and so they do not see it as something to be considered. The younger generation simply does not see the church as relevant to their life and needs. Churches with dynamic music attract the youth who are familiar with ear-thumping, head-shaking music from their experiences with secular pop concerts. Is this the way to attract the youth? Is the unadorned gospel not sufficient to draw them? For a time, the "seeker-friendly church" was in vogue.[20] Here the church offered entertainment such as music and drama. The community would be drawn in, and once in the door, this captive audience would become Christian. Or not.

Loneliness and depression are rampant in our culture. People are looking for some connection with others in society. I have mentioned elsewhere how gangs are the false answer to this need. If the church does not provide the answer, it will not have a chance to proclaim the gospel to such people. Sitting passively in the pew on Sunday morning, shaking hands with the vicar at the door, even having a cup of coffee in the foyer will not provide what lonely people are looking for. They need intimacy, and they need someone to listen to their heart. It will not be found in the hour-long structured Sunday service. Community

[20] Willow Creek Community Church, Illinois, was one of the first to offer a seeker-friendly service.

action has recognised this need by creating men's sheds and other excellent initiatives. It should be Christians who lead such actions.

Many of us are sheltered from the reality of the modern world where poverty is alive and well. If we live in a leafy suburb, we do not see the hundreds of people sleeping rough under the motorway bridges. We do not see the drug-addicted youth begging in the city centre. There are some wonderful outreach programmes that provide for such disenfranchised groups. Some are church-based, and some are not. They may offer food and shelter, or a pathway to freedom from addiction or prostitution. While these are tremendous actions, they do not need to emerge from a religious church-based community. They can just as easily come from house churches or other informal groups. I am saying that such brilliant ministries do not require a functioning denominational church structure as an essential prerequisite. All that is needed is Christians with a passion to demonstrate Jesus' love for the world.

I believe there is a hunger in this generation for a spiritual life. The problem is not a lack of interest in the spiritual dimension. When the church fails to meet this need, there are so many alternatives to lure the unwise into other spheres. The New Age Movement appears to offer many of the same things the church does. It also attracts the Bohemian and the hippie with its way of life. Aggressive proselytising by the Mormon Church and Jehovah's Witnesses lure others away. Those members of society feeling left out or unheard may be attracted to the Muslim faith. Even Paganism and Satanism are finding recruits in such people. There are so many open doors for the spiritually hungry that offer more apparently enticing options than the Christian Church.

The sad truth is that there is a dysfunctional religious church system that actively puts people off the gospel. How sad is that?

REFLECTIONS

We must accept that we are all sinners. But are there aspects of our lives that clearly bring the gospel into disrepute?

Does our everyday language honour the gospel?

Would any of your behaviour put others off the gospel?

Are we intentionally committing any acts that might attract someone to the gospel?

24

THE FINAL DIAGNOSIS

The doctor has identified multiple symptoms. Sadly, there have been so many errors committed by the church over the years. Some have been small, some huge, many unnoticed at the time because they seemed so unimportant. But in the laying of a building's foundation, a slight error in the initial layer of bricks will result in a glaring error at the top of the building. In the preceding chapters, I have tried to show that so soon after the start of the church age (after Jesus' ascension), things began to unravel. And now we need to take down so much of what was inappropriately built and became the Christian religion. Now we need to pull most of the bricks out of the wall before we can start to rebuild. I have called this process "deconstructing" elements of the religious church system. I have also described some of the building bricks that I consider are essential to keep.

Mistakes made by the Israelites foreshadowed what was to happen in the New Testament. After the Israelites had returned from the Babylonian captivity, they immediately began to stray away from God's ordinances. God spoke through prophets at this time. For instance, Zechariah spoke about how a generation had provoked God: "This is what the Lord Almighty says: 'Just as I had determined to bring disaster upon you and showed no pity when your fathers angered me, so now I have determined to do good again in Jerusalem and Judah.'" (Zechariah 8:14-17).

God was saying that if His people corrected their ways and did not fall into the errors of their fathers, He would bless them. In the twenty-first century, we can look back and see what errors our forebears have committed. Small errors crept in during the second and third centuries with the appointment of bishops and other organizational structures. This provided the basis for Constantine to capitalize on the errors and create what was to become the Roman Catholic and Orthodox Churches. Even the Reformation was not able to correct many of the errors that had crept into the *ekklesia*.

The spiritual struggle has not just been about the faith and salvation of the *individual*, but also about *corporate* power and authority. What is the nature of this battle, and who and what are we fighting? It is not people who are our enemy. Paul tells us in Ephesians: "Put on the full armour of God, so that you can take your stand against the devil's schemes. For our struggle is not against flesh and blood, but against the rulers, against the authorities, against the powers of this dark world and against the spiritual forces of evil in the heavenly realms." (Ephesians 6:11-12).

By using the terms "powers of this dark world and spiritual forces of evil in the heavenly realms", Paul is clearly referring to demonic influences working through the rulers and authorities. He experienced this firsthand in the city of Ephesus, as he not only took on sorcery, but the very powerful ruling spiritual authority of the goddess Artemis (Acts 19:23-24).

If earthly rulers and authorities are not submitted to Christ, then they are open to satanic influence. They become prime targets for Satan's highly organised spiritual army – the spiritual forces of evil in the heavenly realms. They are thus no longer neutral but become rulers and authorities under the control of the kingdom of darkness and, as such, they oppose and fight against the Kingdom of God. In other words, they fight against the role and purpose of the Church to be the fullness of Christ in the world.

If the Church is not the fullness of Christ in the world, can we identify why not? I have offered some key elements that I consider are seriously adrift. Are we going to radically mend our ways and anticipate the blessings from God? Or are we going to go on as before, consciously suppressing the knowledge that things are wrong in the *ekklesia*?

This physician is not ashamed to have identified problems in the *corporate* (religious) church system. Even Jesus did that (Matthew 21:12-13, Matthew 23:1-36). I have tried to analyse elements of this religious system and explain why I think it is less than God's desire for us. I am not expecting the world to say "Ah, you are right!" and change the *ekklesia* overnight. Human behaviour is hard to change quickly. Like the Israelites who could not leave the captivity of Babylon because it was easier to stay rather than to face the unknown, many familiar with the life of the local church will find it too hard to leave what is familiar. A pastor may not be able to encourage the break-up of his/her church to be replaced by home churches when his/her livelihood and income might suddenly cease. This reality is especially true regarding the megachurch with multiple staff and a big auditorium to run. It is a big business that cannot easily shut down. The religious juggernaut[21] is pounding along at a nearly unstoppable pace. The reasons it is out of control are complex and not at all wholesome. They include money, pride, power, control, authority, and self-interest. Ouch.

I believe that God is shaking Christianity's religious foundations and will continue to do so until the *ekklesia* reverts to what God desires. I believe the new expression of the *ekklesia* that will emerge will be radically different from the expression of church we are used to.

Is the condition terminal? Not at all. Some of what has been included in this short book so far could be thought of as pessimistic. But I am actually highly optimistic. God has great plans for His *ekklesia*. He has not travelled this far with us to leave us now. No, He has

---

[21] A juggernaut was an enormous carriage that was used to carry the image of the Hindu god Vishnu (whose title was Jagannath, literally "lord of the world") through the streets of India in religious procession. Some worshippers deliberately allowed themselves to be crushed beneath the vehicle's wheels as a sacrifice to Vishnu.

plans for us. This is what He instructed Jeremiah to tell the Israelites in exile in Babylon, a message I believe that is just as applicable to the church in the wilderness today:

> "For I know the plans I have for you, plans to prosper you and not to harm you, plans to give you hope and a future. Then you will call upon me and come and pray to me, and I will listen to you. You will seek me and find me when you seek me with all your heart." (Jeremiah 29:11-14).

ACKNOWLEDGMENTS

While I alone take full responsibility for the final text, I want to acknowledge those who have generously given of their time and expertise to support my efforts. First among equals is Mark Setch who has constantly encouraged and guided me. Chuck Johnson provided professional editing skills. Among those who have been there for the journey include Alan MacKenzie, Mike Yorkey, Raj Perera, Klaus Pluntke, Getahun Gebremedhin, John Karouni, Chris Dickons, Eseta Meneilly, and Marty Gutride. To all the above, my sincere thanks.

ABOUT THE AUTHOR

A medical practitioner whose career has spanned over 50 years; JOHN CLEMENTS has a heart for children in developing countries. His early career included a year running a Christian mission hospital in the Peruvian Amazon followed by postings as Chief Medical Officer in Bangladesh and Afghanistan with Save the Children Fund. He joined the global leadership team for infant and childhood immunization in the World Health Organization (WHO) in Geneva. Over his 17 years with the UN, he worked in around 100 countries, mostly in the developing world. He has taught public health at post-graduate level in a number of universities. He writes extensively and has published many books, book chapters, and articles in the medical literature on public health issues. In 2003 he moved to Australia where he worked as a consultant with several UN and Australia-based international health agencies. He is an associate professor at the University of Melbourne. In 2020 he was awarded Member of the Order of Australia for his work in international health. He has two adult sons, both of whom work in the international aid sector. He has been an elder in an evangelical church for a number of years before moving to house churches.

www.TheGospelUnadorned.com